THE COUNTRY WAIF

GEORGE SAND

THE COUNTRY WAIF

(François le Champi)

Translated by EIRENE COLLIS

Introduction by DOROTHY WYNNE ZIMMERMAN

University of Nebraska Press
Lincoln   London

UNP

First Bison Book printing: 1977

Most recent printing indicated by first digit below:
1   2   3   4   5   6   7   8   9   10

Library of Congress Cataloging in Publication Data

Sand, George, pseud. of Mme. Dudevant, 1804–1876.
  The country waif (François le Champi).

  "A Bison book."
  Text of this edition reprinted from a volume published
in 1930 by Scholartis Press, London, which also included
George Sand's The castle of Pictordu.
  I. Title.
PZ3.S21Cut5   [PQ2402]   843'.8   76–14125
ISBN 0–8032–0888–X
ISBN 0–8032–5850–X pbk.

For a note on the Bison Book edition, see page 5.
Manufactured in the United States of America

INTRODUCTION

THE COUNTRY WAIF is the second of three rural tales—the others are *The Devil's Pool* and *Little Fadette*—which have come to be regarded together with her autobiographical writing as George Sand's finest work. All three are set in the province of Berry, in central France, where Sand grew up and to which she always returned, and all have characters modeled on the Berrichon peasants whom she had known from childhood. She intended to name the series "Stories of a Hemp-dresser,"[1] recalling tales that she had heard as a child, but they were never collected under that title; instead, they are known as the pastoral novels (*romans champêtres*) of George Sand. Although they were written during periods of relative calm when she had returned from Paris to her country house in the village of Nohant, Sand's life during the years 1847 to 1851 was dominated by her political activity and domestic crises; and these tales, while simple in themselves, have behind them much of the complex experience of her extraordinary life. They reflect her childhood in the countryside around Nohant, her

1. *Les Veillées du Chanvreur. Veillées* is almost untranslatable; it means "sitting up late."

youthful romanticism, her later championing of the working classes, and finally her desire to record in fiction that was both poetic and factual the lives of the people and the region she knew best.

Aurore Dupin—George Sand to be—was born in Paris on July 1, 1804. Her father, Maurice Dupin, was a colonel of the Empire who had married Aurore's mother, Sophie Delaborde, only shortly before their child was born. Sophie, in her daughter's words, was "of the vagabond race, a dancer, or rather something lower than a dancer." Yet Aurore was proud of both sides of this mixed heritage—her aristocratic father and her mother who was "of the people."

When Aurore was five Maurice Dupin was killed in a fall from his Spanish charger and she was brought up thereafter by her mother and her grandmother, Mme Dupin de Francueil. Most of her adolescence was spent at Nohant with her grandmother, an aristocrat of independent spirit who believed in the cultivation of the reason and the talents. Her ideas on education were serious, and Aurore was set to studying music—the harp and the piano—and to reading a formidable list of authors. Her father's old tutor instructed her in Latin and the natural sciences. But the countryside was her school as well. She had free range over her grandmother's estate and the fields and woods round about. When tired of study, she knew where to find her *petits camarades rustiques*, and together, as she tells in her autobiography, they disported themselves in the ditches and streams, guarded the flocks (or didn't guard them), and sat in the grass picnicking on country fare—pancakes, cheese, and brown bread. In the autumn evenings they listened to the hemp-dressers who gathered to tell stories while they worked. "Half the village," as she said, came to hear the tales of the old women, which had in them "sometimes the marvelous and sometimes the ridiculous" and all the character of the locality.

Concerned by Aurore's *garçonnière* behavior, Mme Dupin de Francueil sent her to Paris to the Convent Anglais to learn the decorum suitable to her station. At first, as might be expected, Aurore joined *les diables*—the mischief makers—but at the same time dutifully studied the books that were put into her hands. One of these, which she read at the age of fifteen, was the *Lives of the Saints*. Soon after, alone in the chapel, she had a trancelike experience in which she seemed to hear the "take and read" which had inspired Saint Augustine. She read the Gospels (*L'Evangile*), accordingly subdued her ways, and became one of the model girls of the school, even believing she might become a nun. Her grandmother, more alarmed by the saintly than the diabolic phase, removed Aurore from the convent.

Back in Nohant, she was given a horse and

extended her investigations of the countryside to more distant villages. She learned to hunt, wearing a man's shooting coat and cap and tramping over ploughed land and through the woods with a gun on her shoulder. When her mother wrote from Paris admonishing her daughter to be more of a lady, Aurore replied: "You would like me, when I go walking, to lean on the arm of my maid, or one of the other servants. . . . Leading strings were necessary when I was a child . . . . but I am now seventeen, and have learned to walk by myself."

Reading Chateaubriand's *Le Génie du christianisme*, Aurore discovered what she had been looking for—an affirmation of her religious feeling in language that spoke directly to her. She responded to the idea that "in the beauty of the Earth, in Nature and in Love are found the power of life in which God is glorified." Rosseau's *Emile* also spoke to her emotions with its combination of the love of God and nature; she was impressed, too, by Rousseau's sense of justice, his condemnation of the rich, and his faith in the potential of the natural man.

There can be little doubt that the intellectual, physical, and moral freedom Aurore enjoyed in these years contributed to her self-confidence and her belief later that she could survive on her own. Her independent adolescence, remarkable for the second decade of the nineteenth century, laid the foundation for the independent woman she was to become. Between her education within doors and her freedom of action without, she had indeed learned to "walk by herself."

When Aurore was eighteen her grandmother died. She was now an heiress, but also, alas, a ward. Her mother set about finding her a husband but, after various suitors were proposed and rejected, Aurore chose for herself. In 1822 she married the Baron Casimir Dudevant, an officer on inactive duty with an *allure militaire*, and they settled down at Nohant. Two children, Maurice and Solange, were born to them, but the marriage did not prosper, for Casimir took to drinking, seducing the servants, and squandering his wife's money. Eventually, as their mutual dissatisfaction grew, Aurore found companionship and solace in the company of some of the literary-minded young men of the province, among them Jules Sandeau, a writer and student. One day Aurore found a letter from her husband to be opened after his death. Unable to wait for that event, she read the letter to find herself despised and cursed. It was impossible to live with him any longer. She determined to leave Nohant and join Sandeau in Paris; the difficulty was that so long as Casimir was her husband he controlled her fortune. They reached an agreement that she would spend half the year in Paris and half at Nohant, receiving an allowance of three thousand francs. It was barely enough to live on, but off she went.

Aurore's domestic rebellion coincided with rebellion on a grander scale: the culmination of both literary and political revolution in Paris. Full-blown romanticism had come later to France than to Germany and England, but by 1830 Victor Hugo, Alfred de Musset, Eugène Delacroix, and other writers, poets, and painters were proclaiming the reign of love, nature, and liberty, and denouncing tyranny in all its forms. In that same year the people had risen up and toppled Charles X from his throne to make way for the Citizen-King, Louis-Philippe. At this time political refugees from Eastern Europe were pouring into Paris, but far more numerous were the artists, students, and intellectuals who came up from the provinces to the city of light and freedom. Aurore Dudevant was one of the romantic young provincials who arrived in the capital in 1831 on the heels of the revolution. She was twenty-six years old.

Aurore and Jules Sandeau set up housekeeping in a mansard attic apartment on the Left Bank and together wrote a novel, with Aurore doing most of the work. The novel was something of a success, but Aurore, as a woman, received little encouragement in her efforts to enter the fields of journalism and fiction-writing ("Believe me, madame, you would do much better to return to your husband"). Her solution was to take a masculine *nom de plume*—borrowed in part from her friend Sandeau—and thus George Sand was born. Launched into the world of fiction and journalism, from this time on she was always, as she said, "immersed in ink."

Sand's immense literary output (about sixty novels alone) is usually divided for convenience into four phases which match approximately with four decades of her life. In the 1830s she wrote a tempestuously romantic and poetic kind of fiction in which she explored the lives of women through her heroines. In the 1840s, when she was involved in political activity and journalism on behalf of the French working classes, her focus moved away from individual lives to a broader concern for *l'humanité*. The late '40s and '50s were the years of the pastoral novels, in which she abandoned her attempts to deal with the urban proletariat in favor of the peasantry of her own countryside, whom she knew and understood better. In this period she also wrote her autobiography, *Histoire de ma vie*, one of her greatest achievements. During the final two decades her output was miscellaneous, including her letters to Flaubert, one of the best productions of her old age.

Her first major novel, *Indiana* (1832), took up a theme which was also to be the concern of the next two, *Valentine* (1832) and *Lélia* (1833): the unequal position of women in marriage. Though adultery and "all for love" might be celebrated on the stage, the laws governing family relations and the control of property as established in the Civil Code of 1804 (the Code Napoleon) were still intact. Napoleon himself had taken an active part in the formulation of the code, and he considered it important to the order of the state that the old Roman idea of the pater-familias as the controlling agent be fully reinstated. "As the head of the family is absolutely at the disposition of the government," he declared, "so is the family absolutely at the disposition of its head." *Indiana* was a protest against the subjugation of married women. The romantic heroine leaves her domineering husband for an idyllic retreat with her cousin on the Île Bourbon. The exotic landscape in the novel's closing scenes and the tempestuous nature of the heroine reflect the prevailing romantic mode, but in the expression of opposition to the husband's legally sanctioned authority we hear Sand's own voice.

Indiana's success was immense and Sand became the acknowledged queen of the new literary circles. Her friends and admirers included the critic Sainte-Beuve, Liszt, Delacroix, and Alfred de Musset, who became her lover. George Sand's love affairs have been much chronicled and their number exaggerated. She has been variously characterized as a destroying vampire, a nurturing mother goddess, a nymphomanic, and—according to one recent biographer—a victim of nympholepsy. All of these designations are stereotypes and none is very useful. (Curiously enough, it has not been found necessary to give comparable labels to her lovers.) It has also been debated whether or not Sand was a lesbian; the *prima facie* evidence would indicate that she was not. But such issues are beyond the scope of this introduction; suffice it to say that among her most distinguished lovers were Musset, the writer Prosper Mérimée, the radical lawyer Louis Michel, and Frédéric Chopin.

In 1837, Sand began one more novel on the "woman question." Since her arrival in Paris six years before, other women writers had emerged —among them Flora Tristan and Pauline Roland—who were much more polemical than Sand. In reply to these feminists of her day, she began the *Letters to Marcie* in which she intended to expound her position on the status of women. The *Letters*—presumably written to a young girl by a male friend—show a softening in Sand's attitude toward marriage. The essence of her ideas on the institution of marriage is that "those who can receive it, let them receive it." She does not recommend that wives follow her example and leave their husbands; and she has something to say in praise of chastity and fidelity—pronouncements for which Sand has been much taken to task. Coming from one who had had half a dozen lovers in as many years, it is considered a strange, not to say hypocritical, position. But perhaps from her point of view it is not so inconsistent; one might well think that a single "just and good" lover would have been preferable to half a dozen. Romantically, she had always believed in the one true soul mate; was it her fault that she had never found him? The *Letters to Marcie* argue that women are the equals of men, that they should be educated, and that depriving them of education has been one of the greatest crimes of men against women. Sand did not, however, develop her ideas on this subject. Her publisher declined to continue the series, and she may have lost interest in what was essentially a conservative treatise.

Sand did, however, follow her own advice on the subject of fidelity; she met Chopin and settled down to a relationship with him which lasted for nine years. They spent the winters in Paris but almost every summer was passed at Nohant, where, as Chopin wrote in his journal, "My fingers glide gently over the keyboard, her pen flies across the paper." Friends came from Paris and they went on country walks, visited neighboring fairs, attended rural weddings, and collected local ballads.

Sand's novels at this time seem quite removed from the artistic world which she inhabited. She had become interested in social humanitarian politics, and was acquainted with such radical thinkers as the Abbé de Lammenais, who favored Christian socialism, and Pierre Leroux, a printer who advocated a kind of mystical communism. Biographers make much of the influence of these men on her ideas and work, but her concern for the just society had begun long before, with her reading of Rousseau. And she was influenced not merely by radical thinkers but by what she herself observed of the plight of the working class.

Between 1831 and 1851 the population of Paris had jumped from approximately 800,000 to 1,200,000; in some poorer quarters it had doubled. Most of the newcomers had flocked in from the country when work was scarce, hoping to find employment in the city's small factories and workrooms. They crowded into the tenements of the oldest quarters, living in dark, unsanitary cellars and drafty attics, working eleven or more hours a day. Working conditions were miserable, but there was no way the workers could make effective protest. The Revolution had abolished the ancient guilds (*Corporations de Métiers*) along with other remnants of feudalism, and the Civil Code of 1804 legislated against combinations of masters or men. Striking and picketing were criminal offenses, and social services for the poor were almost nonexistent. This "brutal drama" spawned a literature of urban crime from such writers as Eugène Sue, Jules Janin, and even Hugo and Balzac. As for Sand, in such novels as *The Companion of the Tour of France* (1840) and *The Countess of Rudolstadt* (1844) she affirmed a sympathy for and solidarity with the working class.

These two interests—her life with Chopin and her desire to help ameliorate the lot of the poor—occupied Sand during the decade from

1837 to 1847. In the latter year her own life became difficult; she was, she said, under an evil star. Chopin wearied of her political mentors and hangers-on and of her perpetual activity; she complained of his jealousy. Their final break came in July, the rupture made worse by another family problem. Her daughter's husband had proved to be a ruffian and profligate; he ran up immense bills and Sand's Paris house had to be sold. There were scenes, recriminations, and bitterness; and the financial drain was severe.

Work always had been a resource in times of disillusion—"an arm against all regrets and preserver from all annoyance," as Sand had once written to Delacroix. When jarred by the world, she turned also to the countryside where she could "contemplate the sky and the stars . . . breathe the perfume of the wild flowers, and listen to nature sing its eternal idyll." With work and nature to solace her, she began another novel, and in October wrote to her friend Pierre-Jules Hetzel in Paris that she was sending him the manuscript of a new book. It was *François le Champi*.[2]

The serial publication of *Le Champi*, as

2. Titled *The Country Waif* in this translation, *François le Champi* also has appeared in English translations under the titles *François the Waif* and *Francis the Waif*. *Le champi*, a Berrichon word, means "child of the fields." See George Sand's comments on page 25.

INTRODUCTION

George Sand referred to the book, and its interruption by the events of 1848 are described in her preface (see page 7). Although an edition was printed in Brussels in 1848, the authorized first edition was delayed until 1850, when it appeared in two volumes under the imprint of the Paris publisher Alexandre Cadot. In that same year Sand turned the story into a play which achieved some success. The novel itself was popular and went through several editions in her lifetime. *François le Champi* was not Sand's first pastoral novel. It had been preceded in 1846 by *The Devil's Pool (La Mare au Diable)* and was to be followed in 1849 by *Little Fadette (La Petite Fadette),* the three novels forming the triptych of country life which was Sand's most enduring and influential contribution to the art of fiction.

Even before she began writing these novels Sand had contemplated using her considerable narrative skill in the service of a new fictional form and subject matter. In the preface to *The Companion of the Tour of France* (1840) she had written that "there is a totally new kind of literature to be created based on the manners of the people"; and the prefaces to the pastoral novels make explicit her desire to portray country life, manners, and language sympathetically and in a simple kind of narrative. This is a familiar enough conception today, but in mid-nineteenth-century France the lives and manners of rural people were not regarded as appropriate subject matter for fiction. Certainly peasants were not proper heroes and heroines.

She further wished to counteract the image of the poor as dangerous desperadoes. Her preface to *The Devil's Pool* protests against the presentations of poor people as "so ugly, so debased, sometimes so vicious and criminal." In an 1845 letter, complaining of the sensationalism in the novels of Sue, Gautier, and Dumas, Sand asks, "O Sancta simplicitas, where are you hiding?" If Walter Scott and the Abbé Prévost were to return, she said, no one would be able to understand them. The cynicism and brutality of Balzac's novel *Les Paysans* (1844) had offended her, and she wanted to oppose his picture of country life with portraits of *les paysans* as she knew them. Sand believed that something of the virtue of the Golden Age was still to be found in the neighborhood of Nohant. Her readers would be shown "the sky and the fields, the trees and the peasants, especially in what they have of the good and true." The country and the country people provided a model of serenity and a sense of the eternal. She admired Vergil's *Georgics* with their account of the farmer's annual round —sowing, ploughing, harvesting—of the cycle of the seasons, and the weather *varium et mutabile semper*. Like Vergil, she hoped to bring the Muse into her own country.

Sand had long been interested in country tales and ballads; she had tried her hand at transcribing the working songs of the Berrichon peasants and had studied the local dialect. Folk tales and stories told by moonlight or firelight, especially those of the hemp-dressers she remembered from childhood, suggested the form the novels would take. There was some precedent for what she was attempting in English literature: for example, Burns in *The Cotter's Saturday Night*, Wordsworth in *Michael* and other of the lyrical ballads, and Scott in "The Two Drovers" all had made use of folk poetry and rural dialect. Frequently in her letters of the 1840s Sand praised Scott, calling him the "master of us all." Like Wordsworth, she would write some "more humble lay, familiar matter of today."

The landscape described in *The Country Waif*, the story of an orphan boy placed in a rural foster home, has an aura of pastoral, but it is authentic central France. The mill, the old ash tree, the little bridge and pool at the edge of the meadow, while idyllic and beautiful, are also real to the mind's eye. And Sand was scrupulous in her use of local geography. Châteauroux and Mers are not invented; they are a real town and a real village in the vicinity of Nohant. François's return from the Vertaud farm (see pages 115–17) can be traced turning by turning until he comes to the mill on the bank of the Vauvre. The mill does not exist, but the site can be readily identified. The ongoing farm life of the pastoral novels is that of the period. Farming methods had not altered much in hundreds of years, the crop rotation system in central France being that of the Romans. An 1856 observer, Lavergne, wrote that "in Berri . . . things have hardly changed at all since Perette went to market with her milk on her head . . . and the *bonshommes* live on in the old way." The "local habitation" and accuracy of detail in the Berry background have led P. E. Charvet, in *A Literary History of France*, to assert that Sand "created the regionalist novel."

Other elements in the novel have a solid factual foundation. François, as a foundling, was supported—meagerly—under the system of outdoor relief. The *orphelin* of Sand's time was cared for either in an asylum or by a foster parent, usually living in the country, who received a fee. On reaching the age of twelve, the foster child was put to work as a servant or an apprentice. In 1858 there were 93,000 orphans receiving public assistance, and the mortality rate before the age of twelve was very high. In the novel François is one of these *enfants assistés*, living with an impoverished foster mother. When he is found by the miller's wife, Madeleine, he is a sickly child, and quite probably she saved his life by providing food and clothing.

Although Sand's knowledge of the secrets of the countryside has never been challenged, some readers have questioned the validity of her characterizations of Madeleine and François, finding them too good to be true. As a writer Sand understood the importance of "characters real and situations real," but she was also an idealist. She had known, she believed, personalities especially luminous, with an aureole of virtue or poetry, and these were her heroes and heroines in the pastoral novels. It can be argued that the virtuous natures of Madeleine and François are born of their religious feeling, a feeling which also suffuses the novel. They read the *Lives of the Saints* and *L'Evangile* (though we don't hear much of their going to church). Saints' days are noted and observed. Madeleine finds François by the meadow pool near the time of the Feast of Saint Martin, a saint noted for his charity. Something of a saint herself, Madeleine wraps François in her shawl. Crossing the little river with him in her arms, she thinks of Saint Christopher—the name means Christ-bearer—who was said to have stumbled carrying the infant Jesus across a bridge.

The hemp-dresser does not figure in the story of François and Madeleine, but as the chief narrator he orders the language, tone, and action into a simple, unified whole, and his piety shapes and controls the novel. The metaphors are homely and natural: the voices of two angry women were "sizzling and crackling like a fire in a hayloft" and "innocence was as clearly inscribed on [her] face as a prayer in a Book of Hours." The device of the folk narrator saves the novel from the effusions that sometimes emanate from Sand when she begins to write of *le bon Dieu.*

Critics acquainted with the Berrichons have found that Sand's peasant characters ring true. Louise Vincent, in *George Sand et le Berry* (1919), states that Sand accurately caught the religious spirit of the Berry peasants. Mary Duclaux, in *The French Procession* (1909), comments that they are the most lifelike peasants in French fiction, "no less true to life than Maupassant's avaricious Normans. . . . They are peasants of central France, full of gentleness, finesse and feeling, fond of money, full of mutual distrust, ignorant of their real interests, and faithful to routine." Jean François Millet, who began painting the peasantry around Barbizon when *François le Champi* was being serialized, often shows his peasants in pious attitudes. Millet's portraits are rather more solemn and less *joli* than Sand's, and sometimes, as in *Man with a Hoe*, they exhibit a brutishness not present in her novels. But they have lived the same hard life and have the same air of patient endurance as Sand's creations.

Madeleine seems to me a completely believable character. Though poor herself, she displays the same generosity and charity that George Sand believed in and practiced. François in his adolescence is perhaps too pure a youth to be quite credible, but in his manhood when he returns to the mill and sets about putting things straight he displays an admirable and believable energy and character. The novel has many memorable images: Madeleine going home across the fields; Mariette tending her flock under the apple blossoms; François's return to the mill on a bleak winter afternoon.

In *François le Champi* Sand realized her intention of writing a simple story of country life—a romance, not of Arcadia but of a real place, where a dog is in the farmyard and the mill wheel stops turning "when nights are cold and ice is on the river." She succeeded also in her other aim, that of increasing sympathy and understanding between the classes, at least to the extent that she helped in establishing the poor and obscure as worthy subjects of serious treatment in fiction. The same year that the novel began to appear in the *Journal des Débats* Sand went to Paris to support the republicans and proletariat in the Revolution of 1848. Among the tracts handed out from her headquarters were "An Address to the Rich" and "An Address to the Poor," which were attempts to bring the two classes together on behalf of the Republic, of common humanity, and of France. The Republic of 1848 was short-lived and the ideal of political unity failed, but in her pastoral novels Sand made a lasting contribution to that expanding of sympathies which she believed was the goal of art.

Although not flawless, the pastoral novels have been widely praised and influential. Sand's contemporary, Turgenev, wrote that *François le Champi* was "in her best manner, simple, true, affecting. . . . She has the gift of setting down the subtlest and most fleeting impressions in a manner at once firm, clear, and comprehensible. She can depict a scent, even the faintest sound." George Eliot admired Sand, whose influence can be seen in *Silas Marner* and *Adam Bede*; and Flaubert told Sand that he had written *Le Coeur simple* to please her. In our own century, Marcel Proust, who devoted several pages to *François le Champi* near the beginning of *Swann's Way*, said that the novel, though a little old-fashioned, was ever redolent of the "generosity and moral distinction" of its author, and that the pleasant-sounding name of *Champi* "draped the boy who bore it, I know not why, in its own bright color, purpurate and charming." Willa Cather called the pastoral novels "supremely beautiful"; and it is likely that she—as well as Turgenev before her—learned something from Sand about the description of rural scenes.

The pastoral novels were the artistic expression of Sand's deepest emotional experience: the free outdoor life and religious sympathies of her girlhood and the romantic love of nature and regard for the common people which she had learned both from her reading of Rousseau and from her own observation. As a writer she moved from the flamboyance of romantic settings and remote castles concealing Gothic horrors, from chatelaines and scions of noble families, to the familiar terrain and people of her own province. The sense of injustice which engendered *Indiana* and *Lélia* was given broader scope in the defense of the working class. True, the pastoral novels are far from revolutionary in their portrayal of private charity and immemorial patience, but they were motivated by the desire to defend a class she considered unjustly ignored or maligned in the literature of the day. In its movement from the tempestuous and exotic to the simple and familiar, Sand's work exhibits a continuum of romantic feeling which culminates in the pastoral novels.

Her life after the Revolution of 1848 followed a quieter course. She continued to live at Nohant, playing and listening to music, walking in the woods and fields, botanizing, entertaining her friends, reading, and writing; and she enjoyed the esteem of her rural neighbors, who called her "the good lady of Nohant." On her trips to Paris to see plays and to supervise the production of those she had written, she dined with Flaubert, Sainte-Beuve, and others at the famous Magny dinners, where the latest literary developments, including the new realism, were discussed. Her letters to Flaubert tell of the pleasures of her old age: joy in her grandchildren, unconventional daily swims in "this beloved stream," the Indre, and her feeling for "the poetry of country scenes."

George Sand died at Nohant in 1876. Among those at her funeral were Flaubert, Renan, the younger Dumas, and "all the good people of the countryside weeping."

DOROTHY WYNNE ZIMMERMAN

University of Nebraska–Lincoln

BIBLIOGRAPHICAL NOTE

In preparing this introduction I have relied primarily on the following sources:

Cate, Curtis. *George Sand*. Boston: Houghton Mifflin, 1975.

Charvet, P. E. *A Literary History of France*. London: Benn, 1967.

Chevalier, Louis. *Laboring Classes and Dangerous Classes*. New York: Howard Fertig, 1973.

Clapham, J. H. *Economic Development of France and Germany*, 1815–1914. Cambridge: Cambridge University Press, 1963.

Duclaux, Mary. *The French Procession*. 1909; reprinted Shreveport, N.Y.: Books for Libraries, 1968.

Emminghaus, A. *Poor Relief in Different Parts of Europe*. London: Edward Stanford, 1873.

Henderson, W. O. *The Industrial Revolution on the Continent*. London: Frank Carr and Company, 1967.

Maurois, André. *Lélia, The Life of George Sand*. New York. Harper and Brothers, 1953.

Salomon, Pierre. *George Sand*. Paris: Hatier-Boivin, 1953.

Sand, George. *Correspondance*. 8 vols. Edited by George Lubin. Paris: Editions Garnier Frères, 1964–71.

————. *La Petite Fadette*. Paris: Editions Garnier Frères, 1967.

————. *Oeuvres Autobiographiques*. 2 vols. Edited by George Lubin. Paris: Editions Gallimard, 1970.

————. *Lettres à Marcie*. Paris: Nouvelle Editions, 1869.

————. *Oeuvres Complètes*. 110 vols. Paris: Michel Lévy Frères, 1876.

————. *La Mare au Diable. François le Champi*. Edited by Pierre Salomon and Jean Mallion. Paris: Editions Garnier Frères, 1956. It is in this edition that François's route from the Vertaud farm back to the mill is traced.

Vincent, Louise. *George Sand et le Berry*. Paris: Edouard Champion, 1919.

THE COUNTRY WAIF

CONTENTS

3

Contents

A NOTE ON THE EDITION

The text of this edition of *The Country Waif* is reproduced from the original volume in the collections of the Memorial Library, University of Wisconsin. Published in 1930 by the Scholartis Press, 30 Museum Street, London, it also included George Sand's *The Castle of Pictordu*, translated by Philippa H. Watson, and an Introductory Note by Hamish Miles, both of which are omitted in this edition. We are grateful to the Memorial Library for making the original volume available to us.

The Scholartis Press is no longer in existence, and the University of Nebraska Press has been unable to trace the translator, Eirene Collis, in order to determine who holds copyright to this translation of *The Country Waif.* If he or she still exists, we ask that the copyright holder will accept our excuses for proceeding with the reprinting of the work. We wish to acknowledge the assistance and advice of The Society of Authors, London, during our search.

The Scholartis edition did not include George Sand's Preface. It has been supplied in this edition as it was translated by Jane Minot Sedgwick in *François the Waif* (New York: George H. Richmond & Co., 1894).

A NOTE ON THE TRANSLATION

In the Foreword to *François le Champi*, George Sand discusses with R——— (François Rollinat, an old Berry friend), the problem of using the Berrichon dialect in her novel. Her solution was to introduce local words and names and some archaic words into a simple but standard French. Eirene Collis, faced with the problem of translating Sand's version of the Berry *patois*, has wisely not attempted to devise an equivalent dialect, but has translated the story into simple English.

D.W.Z.

PREFACE

François le Champi appeared for the first time in the *feuilleton* of the *Journal des Débats*. Just as the plot of my story was reaching its development, another more serious development was announced in the first column of the same newspaper. It was the final downfall of the July Monarchy, in the last days of February, 1848. This catastrophe was naturally very prejudicial to my story, the publication of which was interrupted and delayed, and not finally completed, if I remember correctly, until the end of a month. For those of my readers who are artists either by profession or instinct, and are interested in the details of the construction of works of art, I shall add to my introduction that, some days before the conversation of which that introduction is the outcome, I took a walk through the Chemin aux Napes. The word *nape*, which, in the figurative language of that part of the country, designates the beautiful plant called *nénufar*, or *nymphoea*, is happily descriptive of the broad leaves that lie upon the surface of the water, as a cloth (*nappe*) upon a table; but I prefer to write it with a single *p*, and to trace its derivation from *napée*, thus leaving unchanged its mythological origin.

7

The Chemin aux Napes, which probably none of you, my dear readers, will ever see, as it leads to nothing that can repay you for the trouble of passing through so much mire, is a breakneck path, skirting along a ditch where, in the muddy water, grow the most beautiful nymphaeae in the world, more fragrant than lilies, whiter than camellias, purer than the vesture of virgins, in the midst of the lizards and other reptiles that crawl about the mud and flowers, while the kingfisher darts like living lightning along the banks, and skims with a fiery track the rank and luxuriant vegetation of the sewer.

A child six or seven years old, mounted bareback upon a loose horse, made the animal leap the hedge behind me, and then, letting himself slide to the ground, left his shaggy colt in the pasture, and returned to try jumping over the barrier which he had so lightly crossed on horseback a minute before. It was not such an easy task for his little legs; I helped him, and had with him a conversation similar to that between the miller's wife and the foundling, related in the beginning of *The Waif*. When I questioned him about his age, which he did not know, he literally delivered himself of the brilliant reply that he was two years old. He knew neither his own name, nor that of his parents, nor of the place he lived in; all that he knew was to cling on an unbroken colt, as a bird clings to a branch shaken by the storm.

PREFACE

I have had educated several foundlings of both sexes, who have turned out well physically and morally. It is no less certain, however, that these forlorn children are apt, in rural districts, to become bandits, owing to their utter lack of education. Intrusted to the care of the poorest people, because of the insufficient pittance assigned to them, they often practise, for the benefit of their adopted parents, the shameful calling of beggars. Would it not be possible to increase this pittance on condition that the foundlings shall never beg, even at the doors of their neighbors and friends?

I have also learned by experience that nothing is more difficult than to teach self-respect and the love of work to children who have already begun understandingly to live upon alms.

GEORGE SAND

Nohant, May 20, 1852

George Sand
By Alexandre Manceau after Couture

FOREWORD

THE moonlight softly silvered the footpaths of the darkening countryside as R—— and I returned from our walk. It was an autumn evening, mild and faintly misty, and we were remarking on the mellowness of the air at that season, and on that elusive sense of the mysterious which then pervades nature. It seems as though the approach of winter's heavy sleep makes everybody and everything furtively agree to enjoy one last fragment of life and animation before the numbing fatality of the frost—and just as if wishing to trick the oncoming steps of time, as if dreading surprise and interruption in the last frolics of their rejoicings, the creatures of nature, animate and inanimate alike, move noiselessly and, as it seems, passively, to their nocturnal intoxication. From the birds come half-stifled cries in place of the gay fanfares of summer. Here and there the insect in the furrows lets out an indiscreet remark—but breaks off at once and quickly goes on to tune his song or his plaint to a different key. The plants make haste to give off their last perfumes, all the more soothing for being so subtle and, as it were, so carefully restrained. The sere leaves hardly dare to tremble in the wind's breath, and silently the flocks browse in the fields without a cry of love or of battle.

My friend and I were walking with a certain cautiousness, and a mood of instinctive tranquillity made us hushed and attentive to the softened tone of nature's beauty, to the bewitching harmony of her last strains as they faded away in an all but imperceptible *pianissimo*. For the fall of the year is a gracious and melancholy *andante* that leads most wonderfully to the solemn *adagio* of winter.

"It is all so peaceful," said my friend at length, for in spite of our silence we had been following each other's line of thought; "it all seems wrapped in a reverie so far removed from and unconcerned with the toils, the forebodings, the woes of man that I wonder how the face of nature we are seeing now could be interpreted in human terms—what expression, what tints, what manifestation of art and poetry. To illustrate my ends more clearly, I would compare this evening, this sky, this landscape, now lying dead and yet so harmonious and complete, with the soul of a wise and religious peasant—one who works and earns, enjoys his own way of living, and is without the need, the desire, or the means of manifesting and expressing his inner life. I, a civilised person, am trying to place myself in the heart of this mystery of simple rustic life. I know not how to enjoy instinctively and am always tortured with the desire to expound my contemplations and meditations to others and to myself.

"And then," continued my friend, "I find it difficult to discover what link there can be between my own brain, all too active, and the peasant's, which is not active enough. And I was brought to wonder just now what can be added by painting, music, description—in short, by the interpretations of art— to the beauty of this autumn night which reveals itself to me in an elusive mystery and enters into my being by I know not what magical channels."

"Let me see," I replied, " whether I have grasped your question : this October evening, that hueless sky, this music lacking in distinct or consecutive melody, this rural peace, that peasant who, by his very simplicity, is akin to us in his tacit enjoyment and understanding—let us group all that together and call it *primitive life*, primitive, that is, in relation to our own elaborate and complex life, which I may term *artificial life*. And you are asking what is the possible relation, the direct link, between these two contrasting states of existence, between palace and cottage, between the artist and the created world, between poet and ploughman."

"Yes," he agreed, "and more exactly—between the language of nature, primitive life and instincts, and that of art, science—in a word, of *knowledge*."

"To continue in your own strain, I reply that between *knowledge* and *sensation* the link is *feeling*."

"It is precisely for a definition of that feeling that I am questioning you in questioning myself. It is he who has the task of interpretation who is troubling me. It is he who is art (or the artist if you like), the interpreter of that candour, that grace, that charm of primitive life, to those who live artificially, and who are, if I may say so, in relation to nature and her divine secrets, the greatest donkeys in the world."

"You are asking nothing less than the secret of art : seek it in the heart of God—no artist can reveal it to you. He does not know it himself, he could not tell the sources of his inspiration or the causes of his

impotence.   How is one to set about explaining beauty,
simplicity, and truth ?   No one knows.   And who
could teach us ?   Not even the greatest artists can do
that—if they tried they would cease to be artists and
become critics ; and criticism ! . . ."

"Criticism," rejoined my friend, "has been walking
round the mystery for centuries without understanding
anything about it.   But, excuse me, that is not exactly
what I was asking.   I am more radical than that just
now : I am questioning the power of art.   I scorn it,
I annihilate it, I claim that art is unborn, that it does
not exist, or that if it has existed its day is over.   It
is outworn, formless, lifeless, with no means for singing
the beauty of truth.   Nature is a work of art, but God
is the sole artist, and man is merely an adaptor in bad
taste.   Nature is beautiful, feeling breathes from her
every pore ; love, youth, and beauty are undying in
her.   But to feel and express them man has only
absurd ways and his feeble faculties.   He would be
wiser not to interfere, to remain dumb and absorbed
in contemplation.   Come, what do you think ? "

"I agree—I ask nothing better," I answered.

"Ah ! " he cried, "you are going too far ; you
are taking my paradox too literally : I am pleading a
cause—respond."

"Very well, I will argue that a sonnet of Petrarch
has its relative beauty which is equivalent to the
beauty of the pool at Vaucluse ; that a beautiful
Ruysdael landscape has a charm equivalent to that
of this lovely evening ; that Mozart sings with the
tongue of men as well as Philomela in that of birds ;
that Shakespeare delineates passions, feelings, and
instincts as vividly as the most primitive and real

16

man might feel them. That is art, that is the link—
in a word, that is *feeling !* "

" Yes—a work of transformation ! But suppose I
remain unsatisfied ? After all, if you were right a
thousand times according to the rules of taste and
æsthetics, suppose I find the cadence of the waterfall
more harmonious than Petrarch's verse, and so on in
each instance ? Suppose I hold that this evening gives
me something that no one could have shown me had
I not partaken of it myself ; and that all Shakespeare's
ardour is cold compared with the passion in the eyes
of a jealous peasant beating his wife, what is your reply?
It is a question of convincing my feelings. Suppose
they defeat your examples and surmount your proofs ?
Art is no infallible interpreter ; one's feelings are
not always satisfied by even the best of definitions."

" Well, I don't know what I can say—unless that
art is a process of demonstration of which nature is the
standing proof ; that the pre-existent fact of that
proof is always there to justify and contradict the
demonstration, and that it cannot be made good unless
the proof be examined in a spirit of religion and love."

" So the demonstration depends on the proof ;
but could not the proof dispense with the demonstration ? "

" Doubtless God could dispense with it ; although
you are talking as if you were not one of us, I wager
you would not understand the proof in the least if
you had not found the demonstration expressed in a
thousand ways in art ; and if you yourself were not a
demonstration continually based on the proof."

" Ah ! that's just what I can't bear. I want to get
rid of this everlasting demonstration ; it chafes me. I

want to annihilate in my mind the lessons and forms of art ; never to think of painting when I admire landscape, of music when I hear the wind, of poetry when I absorb and take delight in the whole. I want to enjoy it all instinctively—that chirruping grass-hopper seems to me gayer and more exhilarated than I am."

" You regret, in fact, that you are a man ? "

" No, I regret that I am no longer primitive man."

" It is questionable if he enjoyed, not having understanding."

" I do not suppose him to be akin to the brute creation. When he became a man he immediately understood and felt differently. But I cannot get any exact idea of his emotions, and that is what troubles me. I should like to be that which society allows a great number of men to be, from the cradle to the grave, I should like to be a peasant—the peasant who cannot read, who is endowed by God with good instincts, a sound constitution, and an upright conscience : I feel that a slumbering of useless faculties and an ignorance of depravity, would give me happiness like that of the primitive man dreamt of by Jean-Jacques."

" Well, I've had that dream, too. Who hasn't ? But that would not prove your reasoning, for the humblest and most ingenuous peasant is yet an artist ; and I even assert that their art is superior to ours. It is a differing form, but it comes nearer to my soul than all the forms of our civilisation. The songs, the narratives, the rustic tales, paint in few words that which our literature can merely amplify and disguise."

FOREWORD

"Then, I am right?" returned my friend. "That art is the purest and the best which arises more directly from nature by being in immediate contact with her. I confess I went to extremes in saying that art is useless, but I also said I should like to feel as a peasant feels, and this I don't retract. There are certain Breton ballads, composed by the beggars, three couplets of which are worth all Goethe and all Byron put together, and which show there is more spontaneous and complete appreciation of truth and beauty in these simple folk than in the most illustrious poets. And music too! Are there not wonderful melodies in our country's music? As for painting, they have none; but they have it in their language, which is a hundred times more vivid, forcible, and logical than our literary tongue."

"I agree," I replied, "and as for the last point especially, I often feel in despair at being forced to write the language of the French Academy when I am better acquainted with another far superior for the rendering of a whole order of emotions, feelings, and thoughts."

"Yes, yes, that naïve world," said he, "that world unknown and closed to our modern art, no study of which, peasant of the earth, will explain you to yourself if you bring it into the domain of civilised art, into the intellectual intercourse of artificiality."

"Alas!" I answered, "this troubles me deeply. I myself have seen and felt, with all civilised beings, that primitive life is the dream, the ideal of all men and all ages. From the shepherds of Longus to those of the Trianon, pastoral life has been a scented Eden where tortured souls sick of the world's tumult have sought to hide. And art, the great flatterer, that obliging solace of too happy people, has passed through an unbroken sequence of pastorals. I have often wanted to write a learned and critical book entitled *A History of Pastorals*, in which I should survey all those different sylvan dreams on which the upper classes have fed so passionately.

"I should trace their variations as being always in inverse relation to the depravity of morals, becoming pure and sentimental as society grew corrupt and shameless. I should like to be able to *command* a writer abler than myself to write this book—and with what pleasure I should then read it ! It would be a complete treatise on art ; for music, painting, architecture, literature in all its forms (play, poem, novel, eclogue, song), fashions, gardens, even costumes—all have undergone the bewitchment of the pastoral dream. All the figures of the golden age, the shepherdesses who were nymphs and then marquises ; the shepherd-esses of *L'Astrée* who passed by the banks of Florian's Lignon who donned satin and powder under Louis XV ; and to whom Sedaine began to give sabots at the end of the monarchy—they are all more or less false, and to-day they seem contemptible and ridiculous to us. We have done with them, we hardly see them save in phantom form at the opera ; and yet time was when they reigned at court, and were the delight of crowned heads, who borrowed their crooks and baskets.

"I have often wondered why there are no more shepherds, for in these days we are not such devotees of reality that our art and literature can afford to scorn these conventional figures, any more than those whom fashion is now setting up. We live in an age of energy and cruelty, and on the canvas of these passions we broider ornaments which, could we take them seriously, would be of hair-raising horror ! "

" If we no longer have shepherds," replied my friend, " if literature has but changed one false ideal for another, might it not be that art is making an involuntary attempt to find its own level, to come within the scope of all types of intelligence ? Will not that dream of equality flung before the people force art to become brutish and fiery, in order to awaken the instincts and passions common to all men, whatever their rank ? We have not yet touched truth. It does not lie in a reality made uglier, any more than in a prettified ideal ; but we are seeking it—that is obvious ; and if we have set about our search wrongly, we are only the more eager to find it. Look how the theatre, poetry, and the novel have substituted the dagger for the shepherd's crook ! and when they introduce rustic life they contrive to give it a certain strain of reality known in old-time pastorals. But there is hardly a trace of poetry in it, I grieve to say, and I see no way of reviving the rustic ideal without painting its cheeks or blackening its scowl. I know you have often thought of doing so ; but could you succeed ? "

" I am afraid not," I replied ; " for I know of no form for it, and my sense of rustic simplicity cannot be expressed in the right language. If I made the labourer use his own mode of speech it would have to be translated for the educated reader, and if I make him talk as we do he becomes an impossible creature, to whom one attributes ideas he could never have."

" Besides, even if you did make him use his way of

talking, your own language would continually contrast unpleasantly with it ; and, in my opinion, you cannot escape this criticism. You draw a peasant girl, you call her Jeanne, and you put into her mouth words she might quite well use ; but you are a novelist, and you would like your readers to share the pleasure you feel in depicting this character, so you compare her to a druidess, to Joan of Arc, and so forth. Your opinions and your language make a discord with hers like clashing colours in a picture ; and one cannot enter into nature under such circumstances, even by idealising it.

" You have since written a better study of reality— *The Devil's Pool*, but I am not altogether satisfied, for *the author* still peeps out from time to time ; you have used " *author's words*," to quote Henri Monnier, an artist who succeeded in portraying the truth in caricature, and who as a result solved the problem he set himself. I know your difficulty is no less real. But you must persevere, even if you don't succeed ; masterpieces are only lucky attempts. So long as you make conscientious efforts you need not bother about creating a masterpiece."

" That is comfort in advance," I replied ; " and I shall begin again as soon as you like ; please give me your advice."

" Well, for instance," he said, " last evening we attended a village gathering at the farm-house. The hemp-dresser told stories until two in the morning. The curé's servant helped and corrected him ; she is a peasant with a little education, whereas he is quite untutored, but gifted and eloquent enough in his fashion. Between them they told us a true story—

rather long, a sort of homely novel. Can you recall it ? "

" Perfectly. I could tell it word for word in their language."

" Yes, but their language needs translating ; it should be written in your *own* language without the use of a single other word unless its meaning is so obvious to the reader as to make a note unnecessary."

" I see : you are imposing a heartbreaking task on me. I have thrown myself into it before, and come out of the attempt dissatisfied with myself, and convinced of my impotence."

" No matter ! You will throw yourself into it again—I know what you artists are ; you are enthusiastic only when confronted by obstacles, and you do things badly if you don't suffer in the doing of them. Come, begin ; tell me that story of the Waif—but not as we heard it together. It was a masterpiece of narration to the minds and ears of us children of the soil. But repeat it to me as though a Parisian speaking the modern tongue stood at your right hand, and a peasant before whom you did not wish to say a phrase or even a word he would not comprehend, on your left. So that you must speak intelligently for the Parisian, and simply for the peasant. The one will accuse you of a lack of colour, the other of a lack of elegance. But I shall be there to judge by what means art, without ceasing to be art, for everyone can enter into the mystery of primitive simplicity and convey to the mind that charm inherent in nature."

" So we are going to make a *study* between us ? "

" Yes, for I shall interrupt you when you stumble."

" Let us sit down on this thyme-covered bank,

and I'll begin. But first you must allow me to steady my voice by going over a scale or two."

"What's that ? I did not know you were a singer."

"I am only speaking metaphorically. I believe one should recall some theme or other to use as a model before beginning a work of art and thus fall into the right frame of mind. So, in order to prepare myself to fulfil your request, I must tell you the story of Brisquet's dog, which is short, and which I have by heart."

"What is it about ? I don't remember."

"It is an exercise for my voice. Charles Nodier wrote it. He tried his voice in all possible keys. To my mind he was a great artist, but he never received all the honour he merited, as so many more of his attempts were bad than good ; still, when a man has created two or three masterpieces, however short, he ought to be recognised, and have his faults overlooked.

"This is Brisquet's dog. Listen."

And I told my friend the story of *La Bichonne*: it moved him almost to tears, and he declared it to be a masterpiece in its kind.

"It should discourage me from my attempt," I said to him, " for that odyssey of Brisquet's poor dog, which took a bare five minutes to tell, is flawless ; it is a pure diamond cut by the most skilled lapidary in the world—for Nodier was essentially a lapidary in literature. Now, I am unscientific, and have to resort to sentiment. Besides, I can't promise to make the story short, and I know before I begin that that prime quality, excellence and brevity combined, will be lacking in my study."

" Never mind, go on," said my friend, tired of these preliminaries.

" Well then," I went on, " it is the story of *François le Champi*, and I will try to recall the beginning faithfully. It was Monique, the curé's aged servant, who began it."

" Just a second," said my critical auditor; " I object to the title. *Champi* is not a French word."

" Excuse me," I replied, " the dictionary calls it obsolete, but Montaigne uses it, and I don't set up to be more French than the great writers who forge the language. Therefore, instead of calling my tale *François the Foundling*, or *François the Bastard*, I call it *François the Champi*, that is, the child left in the fields, as they used to say once in the fashionable world, and as we say hereabouts to this day."

THE COUNTRY WAIF

ONE morning as Madeleine Blanchet, the young wife of the miller of Cormouer, was going to do her washing at the fountain at the bottom of the meadow, she found a child seated in front of her washing-board. He was playing with the straw which served as a kneeling-mat for the laundresses. Madeleine Blanchet, on inspecting the child, was astonished to find that she did not know him. In those parts the roads are unfrequented save by the inhabitants.

" Who are you, little boy ? " she asked the child, who returned her gaze trustingly, but without appearing to understand her question.

" What's your name ? " went on Madeleine Blanchet, sitting him beside her as she knelt down to begin washing.

" François," replied the child.

" François who ? "

" Who ? " repeated the child innocently.

" Whose son are you ? "

" I don't know, I'm sure."

" You don't know your father's name ? "

" I haven't got one."

" Is he dead then ? "

" I don't know."

" And your mother ? "

"She is over there," said the child, pointing to a miserable little cottage, a couple of gun-shots' distance from the mill, its thatch just visible through the willow trees.

"Oh! I know," continued Madeleine, "it is the woman who has come to live here. She moved in last night."

"Yes," answered the child.

"You used to live at Mers ?"

"I don't know."

"You are not a very knowledgable boy. Do you even know your mother's name ?"

"Yes, she is Zabelle."

"Isabelle who ? Don't you know her by any other name ?"

"Of course I don't."

"The bit you know won't do you any harm," smiled Madeleine, beginning to scrub her linen.

"What did you say ?" asked little François.

Madeleine looked at him again. He was a pretty boy with wonderful eyes. "What a pity he is so simple," she thought. "How old are you ?" she asked. "Perhaps you don't know that either."

True, he knew that no more than anything else, but he did his best to answer, being perhaps ashamed that the miller's wife thought him so silly. And he delivered himself of the bright reply, "Two years old."

"I should think so !" retorted Madeleine, wringing out her linen without glancing at him again, "you are a real little goose, and no one has bothered to teach you, my poor child. From your size you must be six at least, but you are not two in wisdom."

"Very likely," replied François. Then, making a further effort as if he were trying to shake off his own stupidity, he said : "You asked me my name. They call me François the Waif."

"Ah ! I understand now," said Madeleine, turning a compassionate eye upon him. She was no longer surprised to see this bonny child so dirty, so ragged, and so entirely given up to the stupidities of children of his age.

"You have hardly anything on," she said, "and it is not warm weather. I dare say you are cold ? "

"I don't know," answered the poor little waif. He was so used to suffering he had ceased to be aware of it. Madeleine sighed. She thought of her own little Jeannie, only a year old, snugly asleep in his cradle, watched over by his grandmother, while this poor boy shivered alone by the fountain. He was preserved from drowning only by Providence, for he was foolish enough to be unaware that if he fell into the water he might die.

Madeleine, who was a very good-hearted soul, took the child's arm and found it hot, although he shivered continually, and his pretty face was quite pale.

"Are you feverish ? " she asked him.

"I'm sure I don't know," replied the child, who undoubtedly had a fever.

Madeleine Blanchet took off the woollen shawl which covered her shoulders, and wrapped it round the waif. He suffered her to do so without showing signs of either surprise or pleasure. She then took all the straw she had been kneeling on, and made him a

29

little bed in which he quickly fell asleep. Madeleine briskly finished washing her little Jeannie's garments, for she was still nursing him and wanted to get home.

When the washing was done she could not carry it all back at once, for wet linen is twice as heavy as dry; so she left the board and some of her things at the water's edge, thinking to herself that she would awaken the waif when she came back. She took up all she could carry to the house. Madeleine Blanchet was neither big nor strong. She was a pretty little woman, proudly courageous, and known for her gentleness and good sense.

As she opened the door of the house she heard a sound of sabots pattering after her on the little bridge over the mill-dam; and, turning round, she saw the waif who had caught her up. He had brought her board, the soap, the rest of the linen, and her woollen cape.

"Oh! you are not so stupid as I imagined," she said, putting her hand on his shoulder, "for you are willing, and no good-hearted person is ever a fool. Come in, my child, and rest. Just look at the poor little thing, his load is heavier than himself! Look, mother," she said to the old wife, who was bringing her daughter-in-law her child, dainty and smiling, "here is a poor little waif. He seems to be ill. You know all about fevers, couldn't you try to cure him?"

"Oh! it's a fever brought on by want," answered the old woman, examining François, "that can be cured by giving him good soup—that's what he doesn't get. It is the waif belonging to the woman who moved in yesterday. She is one of your husband's tenants, Madeleine. She seems to be in want, and I fear she won't pay up very often."

Madeleine did not reply. She knew that her mother-in-law and her husband were harsh dealers and preferred hard cash to charitableness. She put her child to the breast, and when the old woman had gone out to round up her geese she took François by the hand and with Jeannie on her other arm, set off for Mother Zabelle's cottage.

Mother Zabelle, whose real name was Isabelle Bigot, was a woman of fifty. She was as generous natured as it is possible to be when one is destitute and for ever on the verge of starvation. In order to have a little sum coming in regularly each month and eventually to have a young helper in the place, she had taken François, then just weaned. from a dying woman, and had brought him up ever since. But now that she had lost her cattle, she needed to buy more on credit as soon as possible, for she could not make money by means of her little flock and a dozen hens which picked up their food on the common. Until François reached the age of confirmation it would be his job to guard these few creatures at the roadside ; after that, he was to be hired out as swineherd or ploughboy ; and, if he was a good boy, he would give part of his earnings to his foster-mother.

It was just after Martinmas, and when she left Mers Mother Zabelle had left her last goat in payment for her rent. She had come to live in the little cottage belonging to the mill at Cormouer with no other guarantee than a bed, two chairs, a chest, and a few bits of pottery-ware. But the house was in such bad repair, so badly fenced, of such paltry value, that it had either to be left uninhabited or the miller had to take the risk of having wretchedly poor tenants.

Madeleine talked to Mother Zabelle, and soon saw that she was not at all an ill-meaning woman; and that she would do what she could to pay regularly. Madeleine found that the woman was really fond of her waif, but she was so used to seeing him suffer along with herself that the pity of the rich miller's wife occasioned her more surprise than pleasure at first.

When she at last recovered from her astonishment and realised that, far from coming to extort money from her, Madeleine wished to help her she took courage and recited all her story. It was much the same as that of any other poor creature, and she ended by thanking Madeleine effusively for her interest. Madeleine said she would help her as much as she could, but begged her not to tell anyone as she was not really the mistress in her husband's house, and could only help people secretly.

Madeleine then gave Mother Zabelle her woollen shawl and made her promise to cut it up into clothes for the waif that very evening; she was not to let the pieces be seen before they were sewn together. Noticing that Mother Zabelle seemed rather unwilling to cut up a shawl which she would have found comfortable and useful for herself, Madeleine threatened to stop helping her unless she saw the waif warmly clad within three days. "Do you imagine," she added, "that my mother-in-law, who misses nothing, would not recognise my shawl round your shoulders? Do you want to get me into trouble? If you are careful this time I will help you again in other ways.

Now, listen to me, your little waif is feverish and will die if you don't look after him properly."

"Do you really think so?" said Mother Zabelle. "That child is an uncommonly good-natured little creature and it would grieve me to lose him; he never grumbles and is as obedient as a well-born child. As a rule, you know, these foundlings are troublesome little terrors and are always evilly disposed."

"Well, that is because they are despised and ill-treated. If this one is good you can be sure it is because you are good to him."

"True enough," returned Mother Zabelle, "children are wiser than one thinks. This child is not a bit naughty, you know; and, besides, he knows how to make himself useful. Last year when I was ill (he was only five then), he looked after me as well as a grown-up would have done."

"Listen!" said the miller's wife, "send him to me every morning and evening, at the time when I am giving my child his soup. I will make more than enough and François can eat the rest; no one will notice."

"Oh! but I wouldn't dare to bring him to your house, and he hasn't enough sense to know the right time himself."

"Well, I'll tell you what we'll do. As soon as the soup is ready I will put my distaff on the bridge over the dam. You see it can be seen quite well from here. Then you can send the child with a sabot in his hand as if he wanted to get some embers. You will both of you be better fed, for you will be able to eat all your soup yourself if I give him some of mine."

"That's true," replied Mother Zabelle, "I can tell

you are a sensible person, and I am lucky to have come here. If I had been able to go elsewhere I would not have taken your husband's cottage, for, besides the fact that it is in bad repair and he asks a high rent, I was afraid of him ; they say hereabouts he is a hard man. But I see you are good to poor folk and I believe you will help me to rear my waif. Oh! if only the soup would cure his fever ! The worst that could happen to me would be to lose the child ! True, I get little enough out of it, for what the foundling hospital sends goes to keep him ; but I love him as if he were my own son. I know he is a good boy and will help me later on. You know, he is well-grown for his age and he will soon be able to earn a bit."

Thus it was that François the waif was brought up in the kind hands of Madeleine the miller's wife. He soon recovered his health, for he was, as they say hereabouts, " built of lime and sand," that is to say, he had a sound constitution. No rich man in the country could have desired a bonnier or better-made lad for a son. Besides, he was as brave as a grown man ; he could swim like a fish, dive under the mill-dam, and was as fearless of fire as of water. He would leap on the backs of unbroken colts and take them out to grass without even haltering them, spurring them on with his heels and clinging to their manes while leaping the ditches. The odd thing was that he did all this in a quiet unassuming way, without talking about it, and never changing his rather sleepy and simple-minded air. It was this appearance of stupidity which made people think him a half-wit, whereas there was no child more able, sharper, or more sure of himself, when it came to things like dislodging the magpies from the top of the highest poplar, rounding up stray cattle, or killing a thrush with a stone. The other children put it down to the luck which is attributed to waifs in this world. In any dangerous games they pushed him to the front.

" He won't come to any harm," they said, " he is a waif ! Wheaten grain can't withstand the tempest, but tares never get damaged."

All went well for a couple of years. Mother Zabelle somehow managed to buy a few cattle. She did little jobs at the mill and persuaded Master Cadet Blanchet, the miller, to mend the roof of her house where the water poured in. She and her waif were able to dress better, and she gradually lost the miserable appearance she had shown on her arrival at the cottage. Madeleine's mother-in-law certainly made bitter remarks about the disappearance of some little things and about the amount of bread they consumed in the house. Once Madeleine had to take the blame herself rather than let suspicion fall on Mother Zabelle. Contrary to the expectations of his mother, however, Cadet Blanchet did not worry about these things and apparently even wanted to shut his eyes to them.

The truth is that Cadet Blanchet was still very much in love with his wife. Madeleine was pretty without being a flirt ; he was always being congratulated on his choice—and, besides, his business was prospering. He was a person who was hard-hearted only because he feared unhappiness, and had really more regard for Madeleine than one would have thought him capable of. This caused a certain amount of jealousy on the part of Blanchet's mother, and she revenged herself in various unpleasant ways. Madeleine bore this uncomplainingly and never told her husband.

It was certainly the way to stop such things quickly, and no one could have been more patient or more reasonable than Madeleine. But there is a saying in these parts that the results of kindness are less far-reaching than the results of malice, and there came a day when Madeleine was questioned about and scolded for her charitable actions.

It was a year of frozen crops and the river floods had ruined the hay-making. Cadet Blanchet was out of humour ; and one day, as he was returning from market with a friend who had just married a very good-looking girl, the latter said to him : " Well, you had nothing to grumble about either *in your day*, for your Madeleine was also a fine girl."

" What do you mean by ' *my day*,' and ' *my Madeleine was*'? One would imagine we were old ! Madeleine is only twenty now, and I haven't noticed that she has lost her looks."

" Oh, no ! I don't say that," returned the other. " Certainly Madeleine is still good-looking ; but really when a woman marries so young she soon ceases to be admired for her looks. When she has nursed a child she is already worn out ; and your wife was never very strong, as one sees now when she looks so thin and poorly. Is poor Madeleine ill then ? "

" Not that I know of. Why do you ask ? "

" Well, I don't know. She looks sad to me—as if she felt ill or weary. Ah ! women—their beauty lasts but a moment, like the flowering of a vine ! I suppose I shall soon see mine wearing a long face and a grave expression. As for us men, so long as our wives give us cause for jealousy we are in love with them. They irritate us; we shout at them; sometimes we even beat them; that upsets them, they weep; they stay at home, afraid of us—they get bored and cease to love us. Then we feel satisfied; we are their masters. . . . But there comes a day when we realise that nobody envies us our wives, for they have grown ugly. Well, then see what happens! we don't love them any more, and we turn our attention to other people's. . . . Good night, Cadet Blanchet; you were a little affectionate with my wife to-night. I saw it all, but I didn't say anything. However, it will not make us any the less good friends, and I will try not to make her as unhappy as your wife is—I know myself; if I became jealous I should be spiteful; and when I had no more need for jealousy I should probably be even worse. . . ."

A sensible person profits by a useful lesson; but Cadet Blanchet, although an intelligent and energetic man, was too proud to be reasonable. He walked into his house with angry eyes and hunched shoulders. He stared at Madeleine as if he had not seen her for a long while. He noticed that she was pale and altered in looks. He asked her if she felt ill so harshly that she turned still paler and answered weakly that she was quite well. He became angry—Heaven knows why— and sat down to table feeling a desire to pick a quarrel with someone. His opportunity soon came. They were discussing the high price of wheat, and Mother Blanchet remarked, as she did every evening, that they ate too much bread. Madeleine said nothing. Cadet Blanchet wanted to blame her for the waste. The old woman declared that every morning she had caught the waif making off with half a loaf. Instead of getting angry and standing up to them, Madeleine only wept. Blanchet thought about what his friend had said, and that made him even more bitter : so much so, indeed, that from that very day, explain it as you will, he ceased to love his wife and made her life unbearable.

H E made her miserable ; and, since he had never
made her happy, her marriage was doubly
unfortunate. At sixteen she had been married to
this rough, red-faced man who drank on Sunday,
raged on Monday, felt depressed on Tuesday, and on
the following days worked like a horse to make up for
lost time. He was too avaricious to spare a moment to
think of his wife. On Saturdays he was nicer, for he
had done his work and was thinking of to-morrow's
pleasures. But one day of good temper a week is not
enough. Madeleine could not bear to see him jovial,
for she knew that he would come in in a violent rage
the next night. But she was young and sweet and so
gentle that he could not long be angry with her, and
there were still moments when love and a sense of
justice made him take her two hands in his and say :
" Madeleine, there could be no better wife than you.
I believe you were made for me. Had I married a
flirt—I see many of them about—I would have killed
her or flung myself under my mill-wheel. But I
know how good and industrious you are—you are
worth your weight in gold."

But when, after four years of married life, his love
faded, he never had a kind word for her—only contempt
that she took no notice of his ill-behaviour. What
could she have said ? She knew her husband was
unjust, but she considered it her duty to respect the

39

master she could not cherish and never to reproach him.

Her mother-in-law noticed with pleasure that her son had become master of the house again : she said it seemed as if he had forgotten his headship and had not made it felt. She hated her daughter-in-law for being so much better than herself. Unable to find fault, she scorned her for her delicate health, for having a cough in the winter, for having but one child. She despised her for these things, because she knew how to read and write, and because she read her prayers on Sunday in a corner of the orchard instead of joining her and the neighbouring gossips in their chattering and mumbling.

Madeleine commended her soul to God, and suffered resignedly ; she regarded grumbling as useless. She had withdrawn her mind from earthly things and often dreamed of paradise as if she would have found death a pleasant thing. However, she took care of her health and strength, for she felt that her child's happiness depended on her, and she accepted everything because of the love she bore him.

She was not really very fond of Mother Zabelle, but she liked the way in which the woman, half out of kindness and half in her own interests, continued to care for the poor waif. Madeleine, seeing how bad selfish people become, admired only those who were thoughtful for others. But she was the only person in those parts who was entirely unselfish—she was, therefore, lonely and dull, perhaps without realising why.

Little by little she observed the waif (he was then ten years old) falling into her ways of thinking ;

this she gathered from his behaviour—for as to powers of expression, the poor child showed himself no more sensible in his way of speech than on the day she had first questioned him. He had no idea of how to talk, and when anyone tried to chat with him he could not respond, for he knew less than nothing. But when there was an errand to be run he was always willing—if it was a case of serving Madeleine he did it before she asked. Though he seemed not to grasp the request, he performed the act so quickly and so well that even Madeleine was amazed.

One day as he was carrying little Jean, the baby was amusing himself pulling François' hair; Madeleine took the child away from him, saying, with a touch of displeasure, and, as it seemed, in spite of herself: " François, if you begin by letting others take advantage of you you never know where they will stop."

François stupefied her with his reply: " I would rather bear the suffering than return it."

Madeleine looked wonderingly into the eyes of the little waif and saw there something she had never seen in those of more sensible people ; something at once so good-natured and so determined that it quite staggered her. She was sitting on the grass with her child in her lap, and drew the waif down on to her outspread skirt without daring to speak to him.

Madeleine could not have explained even to herself why she felt a kind of fear and shame at having so often made fun of François for his stupidity. True, she had always been gentle about it, and perhaps his silliness had made her love and pity him the more ; but now she felt that he had always understood and suffered from her teasing without being able to reply to it. Then she forgot this incident, for, a little while afterwards, her husband being infatuated with a village wench ceased to care at all for his wife, and forbade her to allow Mother Zabelle or her lad to set foot in the mill.

After that Madeleine thought only of how she could help them even more secretly. She warned Mother Zabelle, telling her that for a time she would appear to have forgotten them.

But Mother Zabelle was afraid of the miller, and she was not, like Madeleine, a woman who would suffer anything for those whom she loved. She said to herself that the miller, being the master, could very well turn her out or raise her rent, which Madeleine could not hinder. She thought that by humbling herself to Mother Blanchet she could get on good terms with her, and that her protection would be more valuable than that of the younger woman.

She went to the old mother and said that in spite of herself—for the sake of the waif whom she could not afford to support—she had had to accept Madeleine's help. The old woman hated the waif solely because Madeleine took care of him. She advised Mother Zabelle to get rid of him—promising to get her six months' credit of rent on that condition.

It was again the day after Martinmas, and Mother Zabelle had no money, for it was a bad year. Madeleine had been so closely watched that she had found it impossible to give her any, so Mother Zabelle bravely accepted the condition and promised to return the waif to the foundling hospital before the morrow.

No sooner had she made the promise than she

repented of it, and the sight of little François asleep on his pallet left her as heavy-hearted as if she were about to do something wicked. She hardly slept a wink ; before daybreak Mother Blanchet came to her, saying : " Come along now, get up ! You must stick to your promise. If you wait until my daughter-in-law has talked you round you won't do it. See ! in her interests as well as your own you must send the boy away. My son has taken a dislike to him for his stupidity and greed ; my daughter-in-law has pampered him too much—I am sure he is a thief already. All waifs are so from birth, and it is ridiculous to expect anything else from such brats. This one will get you turned out of here, he will get you into bad repute ; on his account my son will take to beating his wife one of these days ; and, to crown it all, when he is big and strong he will become a robber on the roads and cause you shame. Come, come, be off ! Take him to Corlay by the field path. The diligence passes at eight o'clock. Get in with him and by midday at the latest you will be at Châteauroux. You can come back this evening. Here is money for the journey, and enough over to have a meal in the town."

Mother Zabelle roused the child and dressed him in his best clothes ; she made a parcel of his other belongings, and taking him by the hand set out in the moonlight.

But as they went along, and as the day lightened, her courage sank ; she could not go fast or talk, and when she reached the road she sat down at the side of the ditch, more dead than alive. The diligence was coming. They were only just in time.

The waif was never in the habit of worrying about things, and up till then he had followed his mother without question. But when, for the first time in his life, he saw a large coach coming towards him, he was frightened of the noise it made, and tried to draw Mother Zabelle back towards the field from which they had just emerged. Mother Zabelle thought he must have realised his fate, and said to him : " Come along, my poor François, it's got to be ! "

This frightened François still more. He imagined the diligence was a big animal, running after him to eat him up. He was very brave in dangers he understood, but now he lost his head and ran screaming across the meadow.

Mother Zabelle ran after him, but when she saw his deathly pallor her courage evaporated altogether. She followed him to the end of the field and let the diligence go by.

THEY returned the way they had come, half-way to the mill. There they stopped, tired out. Mother Zabelle was worried to see that the child trembled from head to foot, and his breast heaved under his ragged blouse. She made him sit down, and tried to comfort him. But she did not know what she was saying, and François was in no condition to understand her. She took a bit of bread out of her basket and tried to make him eat, but he had no appetite, and they sat silent for a while.

At last Mother Zabelle, who always reverted to her first thoughts, grew ashamed of her weakness and told herself that to return to the mill with the child was to bring trouble on herself. Another coach should pass at midday, and she made up her mind to rest where she was until it was time to go back to the roadside. But François had almost been frightened out of his few wits, and, for the first time in his life, he was capable of offering resistance—so Mother Zabelle set about getting him used to the horses' bells, the rolling of the wheels, and the rapidity of the huge coach.

But in trying to give him confidence she said just too much; perhaps remorse made her too talkative; perhaps François had heard Mother Blanchet say something just as he woke up that morning—and that came back into his mind; perhaps his wits

45

were suddenly cleared by approaching misfortune : whatever the cause, he turned to Mother Zabelle with the same look in his eyes that had so impressed and almost awed Madeleine, and said : " Mother, you want to send me away ; you want to take me somewhere far off and leave me there."

Then the words " foundling hospital," which had sometimes been allowed to escape in his presence, came back to him. He did not know what they meant, but it seemed to him even more terrifying than the diligence ; he cried out, trembling : " You want to put me in the foundling hospital ! "

Mother Zabelle had gone too far to draw back. She fancied the child knew more about it than he really did, and, without realising that she would hardly have found it difficult to mislead him and to get rid of him by surprise, she began to explain the true state of affairs. She tried to point out to him that he would be much happier at the hospital than with her and better cared for ; that he would be taught to work, and that he would, for a time, live with some woman, less badly off than herself, who would be a mother to him.

Such consolations only added to the poor waif's misery. The unknown time to come frightened him more than all Mother Zabelle's attempts to show him how badly he fared with her. Moreover, he loved with all his strength that mother who cared for him less than for herself. And he loved someone else nearly as much as Mother Zabelle—and that was Madeleine : but he did not know he loved her and said nothing of it.

He only flung himself sobbing on the ground,

tearing out handfuls of grass and covering his face, like an epileptic. Mother Zabelle, angered and upset to see him in that state, tried to pick him up and began threatening him. François thereupon banged his head so hard on the stones that it bled, and she thought he would surely kill himself.

At this moment Providence willed that Madeleine Blanchet should pass. She knew nothing of the departure of Mother Zabelle with the child. She had been to Presles with wool she had spun. A well-to-do person had wanted it very finely done, and Madeleine was the best wool-spinner thereabouts. She had received the money and was returning to the mill with it in her pocket. She was just about to cross the river by one of the narrow planks, balanced from bank to bank, often used in the fields in those parts, when she heard heart-rending cries, and suddenly recognised the voice of the poor waif.

She ran in their direction, and found the bleeding child struggling in Mother Zabelle's arms. At first she did not grasp what it was about. It looked as if Mother Zabelle had been beating the boy, and was now trying to get loose from him. This seemed all the more probable, for François, as soon as he saw her, ran towards her, and, twining himself about her legs like a snake and clinging to her petticoats, cried : " Madame Blanchet, Madame Blanchet, save me."

Mother Zabelle was a big, strong woman ; Madeleine small, and slender as a reed. She was not afraid, however, and thinking the woman had gone crazy and wanted to murder the boy, she put herself in front of him, determined to defend him or to let herself be killed whilst he ran away.

But the thing was soon cleared up. Mother Zabelle, who felt less angry than sorry, told Madeleine what had happened. From this François understood at last all the misery that it was his lot to undergo, and this time made use of what he heard more sensibly than seemed possible. When Mother Zabelle had finished, he clung to the legs and skirts of the miller's wife, saying: "Don't send me away, don't let me be sent away." And he ran from the weeping Mother Zabelle to the miller's wife, who was even more distressed, uttering all sorts of words and prayers which seemed as if they could not have come from his lips at all—for the first time in his life he was able to say what he willed.

"Oh! my mother, my sweet mother," he said to Mother Zabelle, "why do you want to leave me? Do you want me to die of sorrow because I can't see you any more? What have I done that you have stopped loving me? Haven't I always done what you told me? Have I done anything wrong? I have always looked after our animals, you said so yourself; you kissed me every night and called me your child; you never told me you are not my mother. Mother, keep me, keep me, I pray you as I pray to God. I'll always look after you, I'll always work for you; if I don't please you you can beat me and I will say nothing; but don't send me away until I do something bad."

And he went to Madeleine, saying: "Madame, have pity on me. Tell my mother to keep me. I will never come to your house again if they don't want me there; and when you want to give me things I will know I must not take them. I'll go and talk to Miller Blanchet, I'll tell him to beat me and not to scold you on my account. And when you go out in the fields I'll always be with you to carry your baby, and I'll amuse him all day. I'll do everything you tell me, and if ever I do wrong you won't have to love me any more. But don't let me be sent away. I don't want to go; I'd rather throw myself in the river." And poor François looked down at the river, going so close that it was obvious that his life hung by a thread—that at the word of refusal he would drown himself. Madeleine spoke up for the child, and, though Mother Zabelle wanted desperately to heed her, she saw that they were near the mill—and that was a different thing than being near the road.

"Come along, you bad boy," she said, "I will keep you; but it means that I will be begging my bread by the wayside to-morrow. And you are too stupid to realise it will be your fault that I am reduced to that. That's what comes of taking charge of a child who means nothing to me, and who doesn't even repay his keep."

"That will do, Zabelle," said the miller's wife, taking the waif up in her arms to carry him off in spite of his already considerable weight. "See! here are ten crowns for you to pay your rent, or to move elsewhere if you are turned out of here. It is my money; I earned it; I know they will ask me for it, but I don't care. They can kill me if they like. I'll buy this child. He's mine—not yours any more. You aren't worthy of the care of such a good-hearted boy, and who loves you so dearly. I'll be his mother, and they'll have to put up with it. One can bear anything for the sake of one's children. I would be cut in little bits for my Jeannie's sake ; well, I would endure as much for this boy. Come along, my poor François, you're not a waif any more, do you understand ? You have a mother and you can love her as much as you like ; she will love you in return with all her heart."

Madeleine said these words without really knowing what she was saying. She who was composure itself had completely lost her head for the moment. Her good nature had revolted and she was really angry with Mother Zabelle. François had flung his arms round her neck and pressed her so close that she could hardly breathe, and at the same time he stained her cap and her neckerchief with blood from the wounds in his head. All this so affected Madeleine, so filled her with mingled pity, dismay, sorrow, and resolution that she began to walk towards the mill as bravely as a soldier going under fire. And, heedless that the child was heavy and she so weak she could barely carry her little Jean, she attempted to cross the plank bridge which was quite loose and swayed beneath her feet.

In the middle she stopped. The child had become so heavy that she staggered under his weight, and the sweat ran down her face. She felt as if she would fall from weakness. Suddenly, there came into her mind a lovely and wonderful story she had read the night before in her old book, *The Lives of the Saints.* It was the story of St. Christopher carrying the child Jesus across the river and finding him so heavy that he stopped short from fear. She bent to look at the waif. His eyes were closed, he no longer clung to her ; either from too much grief or from loss of blood, the poor child had fainted.

MOTHER ZABELLE thought him dead when
she saw him thus. Her love revived in her
heart, and, thinking no more of the miller, or of the
bad old woman, she took the child from Madeleine
and began kissing him with cries and tears.

They laid him on their laps at the water's edge and
washed his wounds, staunching the blood with their
handkerchiefs ; but they were without the means to
revive him. Madeleine, pressing his head to her
breast, breathed into his face and mouth as one
restores the drowning. That brought him back to
consciousness, and as soon as he opened his eyes and
saw their concern for him he kissed Madeleine and
Mother Zabelle one after the other so passionately
that they had to stop him for fear he should faint
again.

"Come along, come along," said Mother Zabelle,
"we must go home. No, never, never could I leave
this child. I see that. I won't think of it again.
I will keep your ten crowns, Madeleine, so that I can
pay this evening if I have to. But don't say anything
about it ; to-morrow I will go to the woman at Presles
so that she won't betray us and get her to say, if need
be, that she hasn't given you the money yet for your
work : we shall gain time that way, and I will do so
well, even if I have to beg, that I will soon be out of
your debt, and then you won't be ill-treated because

of me. If you took the child to the mill your husband would kill him—you can't take him. Leave him to me, I swear to look after him as well as ever, and, if we are troubled again, we will think of some other way out."

Fate made it easy for the return of the waif to be silent and secret; for it so happened that Mother Blanchet had just had a stroke—before she could tell her son what she had exacted from Mother Zabelle with regard to the waif. And the most important thing for Miller Blanchet was to get hold of a woman to help in the house while Madeleine and the servant nursed his mother. Everything was upside down at the mill for three days. Madeleine did not spare herself and stayed up for three nights at the sick-bed of her mother-in-law, who died in her arms.

For a time, this shock calmed the miller's ill temper. He loved his mother as much as he could love anyone, and made a point of giving her the best burial he could afford. He forgot his mistress for the time; he even showed generosity to the extent of giving the dead woman's clothes to poor neighbours. Mother Zabelle benefited from this charitable act and even the waif received a few pence. This was because when everyone tried unsuccessfully to obtain the leeches urgently needed for the sick woman, the waif went off and brought some from a pool he knew of without saying a word. And all this in less time than it had taken the others to set out.

Cadet Blanchet almost forgot his rancour and no one at the mill knew of Mother Zabelle's project to send the waif back to the foundling hospital. The matter of the ten crowns came up later, for the miller had not forgotten to make Mother Zabelle pay the rent of her miserable cottage. But Madeleine pretended to have lost them in the fields, running home after she had heard the news of her mother-in-law's accident. Blanchet hunted for them for a long time and scolded fiercely, but he never discovered how the money had been used, and Mother Zabelle remained unsuspected. From the time of his mother's death Blanchet's character gradually changed without, however, improving. He became still less interested in his home, less observant of what was going on, and less miserly in expenditure. He found things less profitable, however, and, growing fat, lazy, and disorderly, he sought luck in dubious transactions, and took to underhand dealing which might have brought in money if he had not had to pay out with one hand what he earned with the other. His mistress dominated him more every day. She took him to fairs and other gatherings to cheat and trick; they frequented taverns; he learnt to gamble and was often lucky. He had better have lost and thus been sickened of it—for this profligacy proved his undoing—and the least loss made him furious with himself and evilly disposed towards everyone else.

Whilst living this depraved life his wife, always good and sweet, remained at home and brought up their only child lovingly. She looked upon herself as a mother twice over, for she had grown to love the waif very dearly and watched over him almost as much as over her own son. And the more dissolute her husband became, the less she slaved and the happier she grew. At the beginning of his period of debauch he still showed his churlishness, for he was afraid of reproaches and wanted his wife to remain frightened and submissive. When he saw that it was her nature to detest quarrelling, and that she was not jealous, he decided to leave her alone. As his mother was no longer there to excite him against her, he was able to realise that he could not have had a less exacting wife than Madeleine. He used to be away from home for weeks at a time, coming in one day in the mood to make a scene. His anger died under the patient silence with which she met him ; at first he used to be astonished, but in the end he went straight to sleep. In fact, he was not seen at home except when he was tired and needed repose. To live thus alone with an old maid and two children demanded of Madeleine a Christian spirit, which was perhaps more evident in her than in many a nun. In allowing her to learn to read, and understand what she read, God had been very good to her. She was forced, however, always to read the same things, for she had but two books—the Holy Gospel and an abridged edition of the *Lives of the Saints*. The Gospel comforted her and made her weep as she read it alone by her son's bedside in the evenings. The *Lives of the Saints* had another effect on her, like the stories read by people who have nothing better to do— stories which fill their heads with imaginings and day-dreams : not that it was really comparable with them, for these stories all gave Madeleine courage and even made her gay. Sometimes in the fields the waif would see her smiling and flushed when the book lay on her lap. This amazed him. He found it hard to realise that the stories which she took the trouble to recite to him, adapting them a little to his understanding (partly also perhaps because she did not altogether understand them herself), could come out of that thing she called a book. He desired to learn to read too, and learned so well and so quickly that Madeleine was astonished. By and by, he was able to teach little Jean. When François reached the age of confirmation Madeleine helped him to learn the catechism ; and the curé of their parish was very pleased with the quick wits and good memory of the child, who, however, always passed for a simpleton in the village on account of his slow speech and his timidity. After his first communion, as he was old enough to go into service, Mother Zabelle was glad to send him to the mill. Miller Blanchet made no objection, for it was now clear to everyone that the waif was a good boy, industrious and willing, and stronger, more alert, and more sensible than the other children of his age. Also it was an economy to employ a lad who only asked ten crowns as wages. François was extremely happy to be altogether in the service of Madeleine and his dear little Jeannie, of whom he was very fond. When he realised that the money he earned would pay Mother Zabelle's rent and take a big load off her mind he felt as rich as a king.

Unhappily, poor Mother Zabelle had not long to enjoy this reward. At the beginning of the year she became very ill, and in spite of all the care of the waif and of Madeleine she died on Candlemas Day, after having appeared so much better that they thought her cured. Madeleine regretted her loss and wept a great deal, but she tried to console the poor waif who, had it not been for her, would not have survived this grief.

A year later he was still thinking of her every day and nearly every minute of the day, and once he said to the miller's wife :

"When I pray for the soul of my poor mother I feel a sort of repentance : for this reason—I feel I did not love her enough. I am certain I always did my utmost to please her ; I never said any but kind words to her, and I served her in all things as I serve you. But I must confess something to you, Madame Blanchet, something which troubles me and for which I often ask pardon of God. It is that ever since the day my poor mother wanted to send me back to the orphans' home, and when you took my part and prevented her, my love for her grew less in my heart in spite of myself. I didn't want it to—I would not even allow myself to think she had done wrong in wanting to forsake me. It was quite right ; I was in the way, she feared your mother-in-law, and actually it was against her own inclinations, for indeed I saw she loved me very much. I don't know how it is—the idea keeps running in my mind and I cannot get rid of it. From the moment you said those words which I shall never forget, I loved you better than her ; and do what I might I thought more often of you than of her. Well, she is dead, and I am not dead of grief, as I should be if you died."

"What were the words I said, my poor child, to make you give me so much affection ? I don't remember them."

"You don't remember them ? " said the waif sitting at Madeleine's feet—she was spinning at her wheel as she listened to him. "Well, when you gave my mother the money you said, 'See ! I'll buy that child from you ; he is mine.' And you kissed me and said, ' Now you are no longer a waif, you have a mother who loves you as dearly as if she had brought you into the world.' Didn't you say that, Madame Blanchet ? "

" Very likely. I said what I felt and I feel it still. Do you think I have not kept my word ? "

" Oh no,—only——"

" Only what ? "

" No, I won't say. It is wrong to grumble, and I don't want to be ungracious and ungrateful."

" I know you can't be ungrateful, and I want you to tell me what you have on your mind. Come, what is it that you need to be my child ? Say. I order you to tell me as I would order Jean."

" Well—it's—it's that you often give Jeannie a kiss and you have never kissed me since the day we were just talking of. And I always take care to keep my face and hands clean because I know you don't care for dirty children, and you are for ever washing Jeannie and combing his hair. But you don't kiss me any the more for that, and my mother Zabelle hardly ever did either. And I see all the other mothers caress their children, and for that I know I am still a waif and you can't forget it."

" Come and kiss me, François," said the miller's wife, taking the child into her lap and kissing his forehead with much emotion. " I was wrong never to think of it, and you deserved more from me. Look—you see how lovingly I kiss you, and now you are quite sure you are no longer a waif, aren't you ? "

The child flung his arms round Madeleine's neck and grew so pale that she was surprised. She gently lifted him down from her knee, trying to distract his attention. But after a moment he was off like a flash, dashing away to hide somewhere. This worried the miller's wife and she went to look for him. She found him on his knees in a corner of the barn.

"Come, come, François," she said, lifting him to his feet, "I don't know what's wrong with you. If you are thinking of poor Mother Zabelle, just say a prayer for her and you will feel calmer."

"No, no," said the child, twisting the hem of Madeleine's overall in his fingers and kissing it with all his strength; "I'm not thinking of my poor mother. Aren't you my mother?"

"What are you crying for, then? You make me unhappy."

"Oh, no! oh, no; I'm not crying," replied François, quickly wiping his eyes and brightening up. "That is—I don't know why I'm crying. Truly, I don't know, for I am as happy as if I were in heaven."

FROM that day Madeleine kissed the child night and morning—neither more nor less than as if he had been her own, and the only difference she made between Jeannie and François was that the younger was the more spoiled and petted, as became his age. He was only seven, whereas the waif was twelve, and François understood quite well that a big boy of his age could not be pampered like a baby. Besides, they were even more different in appearance than in age. François was so big and strong, he passed for fifteen; and Jeannie was small and slender like his mother, whose timidity he had inherited as well. In fact, one morning, when François arrived and she greeted him on the doorstep as usual with a kiss, the servant said to her :

"To my mind—begging your pardon, ma'am—the lad is too big to let himself be kissed like a little girl."

"Do you think so ? " answered Madeleine in surprised tones. " But don't you know how old he is ? "

"Indeed, I do. I wouldn't see any harm in it either, save that he is a waif. Why, I, who am only your servant, wouldn't kiss *that* creature for a good deal."

"What you say is wrong, Catherine," replied Madame Blanchet ; "and, above all, you had no business to say it in front of the poor child."

"Let her say it, and let the whole world say it!"
retorted François stoutly, "I don't care. As long as
I am not a waif to you, Madame Blanchet, I am very
happy."

"My word! listen to that," said the servant.
"That's the first time I've heard him speak at such
length. Then you do know how to string three words
together, eh, François? Well, I really thought you
hadn't an idea of what one said. If I had known you
were listening I wouldn't have said what I did in
front of you, for I don't want to hurt your feelings.
You are a good boy, quiet and obedient. Come,
don't think any more about it; if I think it queer that
our mistress kisses you it is because you seem to me
too big for that sort of thing, and that your coaxing
ways make you look sillier than you really are."

Having thus remedied the matter, the big woman
went off to make the soup and thought no more about
it. But the waif followed Madeleine to the washing
place and, sitting down beside her, went on talking
as if to her, and to her only, he knew how to talk.

"Do you remember, Madame Blanchet," he asked,
"once I was here, a long while ago, and you put me
to sleep wrapped up in your shawl?"

"Yes, my child," she replied; "and that was the
first time we saw each other."

"It was the first time, was it? I wasn't sure. I
don't remember it very well, for when I think about
that time it seems like a dream. How many years
ago is it?"

"It is—wait a bit—it is about six years ago, because
my Jeannie was just fourteen months old."

"At that rate, I wasn't as old then as he is now.

Do you think that when the time comes for him to make his first communion he will remember all that happens now ? "

" Oh yes, I will easily remember," said Jeannie.

" It depends," went on François. " What were you doing this time yesterday ? "

Jeannie, surprised, opened his mouth to reply, and instead looked sheepish.

" Well, and you? I'll bet you don't know either," said the miller's wife to François. She often amused herself listening to their chatter.

" I, I ? " said the waif, embarrassed. " Wait a minute now. . . . I went to the fields, I came this way . . . and I thought about you ; it was exactly yesterday that I remembered the day you wrapped me in your shawl."

" You have a good memory, it is surprising that you can remember as far back. And do you remember that you had a fever ? "

" No, indeed."

" And that you brought my linen to the house without being told ? "

" No."

" I have always remembered, because by that I knew how good-natured you were."

" And I, aren't I good-natured, mother ? " asked little Jeannie, offering his mother the half-eaten apple he held.

" Certainly you are ; and all the good things you see François do you will do later on."

" Yes, yes," replied the child quickly. " I will get on the bay colt and take it to pasture."

" I believe you ! " laughed François, " and will you

climb up the big apple tree, and rout the tom-tits out of their nests ? You wait, little silly, till I let you do it. But tell me, Madame Blanchet, I want to ask you something ; but I don't know if you will mind telling me."

" Let me hear it."

" It is—why do they think they will make me angry by calling me a waif. Is it a bad thing to be a waif ? "

" Of course not, my child. It is not your fault."

" Whose fault is it, then ? "

" It is the fault of the rich."

" The rich ! How's that? "

" You're asking me a lot of questions to-day. I will tell you that later on."

" No, no ; at once, Madame Blanchet."

" I can't explain it to you. . . . First of all, do you yourself know what it is to be a waif ? "

" Yes ; it is to have been put in the foundling hospital by your father and mother because they haven't the means of feeding you and of bringing you up."

" That's it ; you see, then, that if there are people so miserably poor that they cannot bring up their children themselves it is the fault of the rich who won't help them."

" Ah ! so it is," answered the waif thoughtfully. " All the same, there are good rich people, for you are one, Madame Blanchet ; all one needs is to have the luck to meet them."

The waif, who, ever since he learnt to read and made his first communion, went about musing and seeking reasons for everything, pondered on what Catherine had said to Madame Blanchet. But it was no use thinking—he could never understand why, because he was growing up, he should not kiss Madeleine. He was the most innocent of boys, and never dreamt of things that lads of his age in the country learn all too quickly. His extreme chastity of mind arose from the fact that he had not been brought up like the others. Because he knew he was a foundling he always felt timid rather than ashamed ; and although not feeling it an insult to be called a waif, yet he never got over his astonishment at being different in this respect from everyone about him. Other waifs are almost always humiliated by their lot, and this lot is so early brought home to them that they lose their Christian spirit, and grow up detesting those who brought them into the world, and equally hating those who keep them there. But, as it happened, François had fallen into the hands of Mother Zabelle who loved him and did not ill-treat him, and then he had met Madeleine who was the kindest and most thoughtful creature in the world. She had been to him neither more nor less than a good mother, and a waif who meets with affection is better than other children, just as he is worse when he is bullied and humiliated. François had only found amusement and contentment in Madeleine's company, and instead of playing with the other shepherd boys he grew up solitary or in the company of the two women who loved him. With Madeleine especially he felt as happy as Jeannie could feel, and he had no inclination to seek the company of those who treated him as a waif and with whom he imme-diately felt, without knowing why, a stranger. He reached the age of fifteen without any knowledge of wrong or any conception of evil, with innocent lips, and ears deaf to bad words. Moreover, since the day when Catherine had criticised her mistress for the affection she showed him, the child had had the good sense and acute judgment to refrain from the caresses of the miller's wife. He appeared never to think of it, and perhaps he felt ashamed to behave like a little girl and a coaxer as Catherine said. But, at bottom, it was not shame which restrained him ; and he would have laughed at the idea had he not guessed that the woman he so dearly loved might be reproached for it. Why reproached ? He could not explain ; and, although he would never be able to find out for himself, he shrank from asking Madeleine to explain it. He realised that she was capable of bearing criticism because she was affectionate and good-natured ; for he had a good memory, and remembered that Madeleine had been scolded and in danger of a beating at times for her kindness to him. So that he instinctively avoided being the cause of any revival of her embarrassment. He understood. It is extraordinary, but this poor child understood that a waif has the right only to be loved secretly, and sooner than cause unpleasantness to Madeleine, he would have consented not to be loved at all.

He was reliable at his work, and as he grew older and had more on his hands he saw less of Madeleine. But he did not grieve over this, for he told himself that he was working for her sake and that he would be rewarded by a sight of her at meals. In the evening when Jeannie was asleep and Catherine gone to bed, François stayed up for an hour or two and read or talked to Madeleine as she worked. Country-folk do not read quickly, so that the two books they had were enough to content them. To read three pages in an evening was a great deal, and when the book was finished a sufficient time had elapsed since the first page for them to begin again without remembering too much of it. Besides, there are two ways of reading, and people who think themselves well-educated should remember that. Those who have plenty of time to themselves and numbers of books imbibe all they can and cram their heads until they are thoroughly confused. Those who have neither time nor libraries are glad when a good book falls into their hands. They read it over a hundred times without wearying of it, and each time something strikes them which they had missed before. At bottom, it is the same notion, but it is so pondered, so well savoured and digested, that the one mind is better nourished and in better condition for that bit alone than thirty thousand brains filled with air and snippets of knowledge. What I am saying to you, my children, I got from the curé, and he knows what he is talking about.

Well, these two people were content with what they had to consume in the way of knowledge; they consumed it slowly, helping one another to understand and love that which renders us just and good. In that way they acquired a fine religion and a great courage. They knew no greater happiness than to feel themselves at one with the whole world, and to agree at all times and in all places on the subject of truth and the desire to do right.

MILLER Blanchet was no longer so mean over household expenditure, for he set aside the smallest possible sum each month and gave it to his wife. Madeleine could, without annoying him, go short herself and give to those around her whom she knew to be more necessitous than herself. One day a bit of wood, another, half her meal, yet another, vegetables, linen, eggs, and so on. She did her utmost for her neighbours, and when means failed her, she did the work of these poor folk with her own hands and saved them from dying of sickness or overwork. She was economical and mended her garments so carefully that she appeared well-to-do; and besides, as she did not want her own family to suffer for her charity, she fell into a habit of eating practically nothing, never resting, and sleeping as little as possible. The waif observed all this and thought it quite natural; for, of his own accord, as much as by Madeleine's instruction, he felt the same inclination and was drawn toward the same duty. But he grew anxious at the exertions of the miller's wife, and accused himself of sleeping and eating overmuch. He wished he could spend the night sewing and spinning in her stead, and when she wanted to pay him his wages, which had risen to nearly twenty crowns, he became annoyed and insisted on her keeping them, unbeknown to the miller.

" If my mother Zabelle were alive," he said, " that money would be hers. Whatever can I do with money ? I have no need of it, for you look after my clothes and provide me with sabots. Keep it, then, for those less fortunate than I. You do so much already for poor folk ! Well, if you give me money, you will have to work still more ; and if you were to fall ill and die like my poor Zabelle, whatever good would it be to me to have a full money-box ? Would it bring you back, or prevent me from throwing myself into the river ? "

" You don't think what you're saying, my child," Madeleine said to him one day as he spoke again of this idea. " To kill oneself is unchristian, and if I died it would be your duty to go on living to console and support my Jeannie. Well, wouldn't you do it ? "

" Yes, so long as Jeannie remained a child and needed my friendship. But afterwards. . . . Don't let's talk of it, Madame Blanchet. I can't be a good Christian in that respect. Don't tire yourself out and die if you want me to go on living on earth."

" Don't worry about it, I have no desire to die, I am quite well. I am hardened to work, and nowadays I am stronger than I used to be in my youth."

" In your youth ! " said François, astounded. " Aren't you young still ? "

And he feared she might be of an age to die.

" I don't believe I ever had time to be young," answered Madeleine, laughing like someone putting a good face on misfortune ; " and now I am twenty-five —an age which begins to tell on a woman of my constitution : for I was not born robust like you, little one, and my troubles have made me feel older than I am."

"Troubles! Yes, good heavens! I noticed it when Miller Blanchet used to speak to you so severely. Oh! God forgive me—I am not really bad, but one day when he raised his arm as if to strike you—oh! it was well for him he refrained, for I had seized a flail in my hand—nobody was looking—and I was just about to fall on him with it. But that is ages ago, Madame Blanchet, for I remember that I was a whole head shorter than he and now I can see over *his* head. Nowadays, Madame Blanchet, he says hardly anything to you; and you aren't unhappy, are you? '

" So you think I am no longer unhappy, do you? " said Madeleine a little sharply, thinking that she had never known love in her marriage. But she checked herself, it was nothing to do with the waif and it was not right to put such ideas into a child's head. " You are right," she said, " I am not unhappy any longer : I live as I please. My husband is much kinder to me ; my son is getting on well and I have nothing to complain of."

" And I? You don't include me in your reckoning? I . . . I . . . "

" Well, you are getting on nicely too and that gives me much pleasure."

" Don't I please you, in any other way, though? "

" Yes, you are well-behaved, you are sensible about everything, and I am very pleased with you."

" Oh, if you were not satisfied with me, what a queer fellow, what a good-for-nothing I should be after all you have done for me. But there is something else which ought to make you happy if you think as I do."

" Well, tell me ; for I can't imagine what mystery you are getting up to surprise me."

" No mystery, Madame Blanchet. I have only to examine myself and I see something ; that is, that even if I suffered from hunger, thirst, heat, or cold, and if I were beaten nearly to death every day into the bargain ; suppose I had no more than a bundle of thorns or a heap of stones for a bed—Well, . . . do you see what I mean ? "

" I think so, my François ; you wouldn't be unhappy in spite of all that misery, provided your heart was at peace with God."

" There's that, and that goes without saying. But I really meant something else."

" I don't follow you ; I see you are cleverer than I am."

" No, I'm not clever. I mean I would endure all the pains a man living this mortal life might have to bear, and would still be happy in thinking that Madeleine Blanchet is fond of me. And that's why I said just now that if you thought the same, you would say François loves me so much I am glad to be alive."

" You are right, my dear boy," replied Madeleine ; " and the things you say sometimes make me feel like weeping. Yes, truly your affection for me is one of the joys of my life, and perhaps the greatest after . . . No, I mean *with* my Jeannie's. As you are older than he is you understand better what I say, and you can tell me your own thoughts better. I assure you I never feel weary with you two, and I ask only one thing of God now, and that is that we may stay long as we are without being parted."

" Without being parted, I should hope so ! " said François. " I would rather be cut in bits than leave you. Who else would love me as you do ? Who else would risk being ill-treated for the sake of a poor waif and call him her child, her dear son—for you often, nearly always, call me that. And when we are alone you often say : Call me 'mother' and not always Madame Blanchet. But I daren't, because I am afraid of falling into the habit and of letting it out in front of somebody."

"Well, what of it ? "

"Oh, they would grumble at you, and I don't want you to get into trouble on my account. I'm not proud, I tell you. I don't care if no one knows you have raised me from being a waif. It makes me happy enough to know for myself that I have a mother whose child I am. Oh, you mustn't die, Madame Blanchet," added poor François, gazing sadly at her, for he had felt unhappy about this for some time. " I wouldn't have anybody on earth who cared for me if I lost you ; you would go to Heaven and I am not sure that I am fit to follow you there."

In all he said and thought François seemed to have a presage of ill, and a short while after this ill befell him.

He had become the miller's assistant. He went on horseback to fetch the grain from the customers and took it back to them ground to flour. That meant he often had long journeys to make and that he went to Blanchet's mistress who lived a couple of miles from the mill. He disliked this particular errand, and never stayed a minute in the house after his corn had been weighed and measured. . . .

·   ·   ·   ·   ·

At this point the story-teller stopped.

"Do you realise how long I have been speaking ? "

she asked the listening villagers. "I haven't such good lungs as I had at fifteen, and it's my opinion that the hemp-dresser knows the facts better than I, and could well take up my story. Especially as I have come to a part I don't remember so well."

"I know well why your memory has become defective in the middle of the tale," said the hemp-dresser, "it is because the waif began to have bad luck just then, and that upsets you; for, like all pious folk, you are soft-hearted over love stories."

"Is it going to turn into a love story, then?" asked Sylvine Courtioux, who happened to be there.

"Ah! there you are!" cried the hemp-dresser, "I knew very well that word would make the young ladies prick up their ears. But be patient, the place where I take up the tale in order to lead up to a happy ending does not tell you what you want to hear. Where did you stop, Mother Monique?"

"It was about Blanchet's mistress."

"Ah, that's right," said the hemp-dresser. "This woman was named Sévère, but her name was not very suitable, for there was nothing like that in her make-up. She knew very well how to wheedle the men when she wanted to see the glint of their money in the sun. You couldn't call her wicked, for she was of a jolly and care-free nature, but she kept all her gains for herself and never bothered about anyone else so long as she was smartly dressed and made much of. She had been the rage in those parts, and it was said that she found too many folk to her liking. She was still a good-looking woman, very attractive and lively, though rather plump, and rosy as a cherry. She took little notice of the waif, and if she chanced to meet

71

him in her barn or yard she twitted him without ill-will, just for the amusement of seeing him blush, for he blushed like a girl and felt uncomfortable whenever she addressed him. He thought her bold, and she seemed to him ugly and evil, although she was neither in reality : at least her ill-temper only appeared when she was crossed in her affairs, or when her vanity was ruffled : and it is only fair to say that she liked to give as well as to receive. She was ostentatiously generous and enjoyed receiving people's gratitude. But to the waif's way of thinking only a devil could reduce Madame Blanchet to such poverty and drudgery.

When, however, the waif was in his seventeenth year Madame Sévère discovered that he was extremely handsome. He did not resemble the other country children who are thick-set and dumpy at that age, and only develop into something worth looking at two or three years later. He was tall and well-made, with a white skin, even at harvesting time, and curly hair, dark at the roots and golden on top.

(Do you like that kind, Madame Monique—the hair, I mean, not the boy ?

" Mind your own business ! " retorted the curé's servant, " and get on with the story.")

He was always poorly dressed, but he loved cleanliness as Madeleine Blanchet had taught him to be clean ; and he had an air about him which the others had not. Madame Sévère gradually realised this, and she was so well aware of it in the end that she resolved to draw him out a bit. She had no prejudices, and when she heard people say, " It is a shame such a handsome boy should be a waif," she answered : " Waifs have every reason to be beautiful, for they are love-children." She devised the following plan to get him to herself. She made Blanchet drunk at the fair at St. Denis-de-Jouhet, and when she saw he was incapable of staggering home she sent him to bed at a friend's house near by. Then she said to François, who had come with his master to drive the cattle to the fair, " I'll leave my mare for your master to get home on to-morrow, my boy ; you had better ride his and take me on the pillion as far as my house."

This idea was not at all to François' taste. He protested that his master's mare was not strong enough to carry two people, and he offered to escort Madame Sévère, she on her animal and he on Blanchet's ; he said he would return immediately with another horse and take good care to be at St. Denis-de-Jouhet early the next morning : but Madame Sévère took no heed of him and ordered him to obey her. François was afraid of her, for as Blanchet did all she said she could have got him dismissed from the mill if he offended her—especially as it was near St. John's term. He took her on his pillion, thinking, poor lad, that it was the best way out of the difficulty.

WHEN they set out it was dusk, and when they reached the sluice-gate of the pool at Rochefolle it was pitch dark. The moon had not risen above the trees, and in those parts the roads are cut up by the springs and are not at all good. But François spurred the mare and went fast, for he was sick of Madame Sévère and longed to be with Madame Blanchet.

But Madame Sévère, who was in no hurry to reach her destination, began to act the fine lady and to say that she was afraid and that the mare ought to walk for she could hardly lift her feet and risked falling on her knees.

" Bah ! " returned François without paying any attention, " that would be the first time she said her prayers, for I never saw a less pious mare ! "

" You are very witty, François," giggled Madame Sévère, as though François had said something new and amusing.

" Indeed I am not," replied the waif, thinking she was making fun of him.

" Come, you aren't going to let her go downhill at a trot, I should hope."

" Don't get alarmed ! I intend to take it at the trot."

Their speed made the buxom Madame Sévère quite breathless and prevented her from talking.

74

This vexed her for she counted on wheedling the young man. But she did not want him to see that she was neither young enough nor slight enough to endure the strain, so she held her tongue for a while. When they reached a chestnut wood, however, she bethought herself of saying.:

" Stop, François ; you'll have to get down, my dear François ; the mare has cast a shoe ! "

" Even if she had," retorted François, " I have neither hammer nor nails to re-shoe her."

" But you mustn't lose the shoe. They cost a lot. Get down, I tell you, and look for it."

" By Jove ! I could search a couple of hours without finding it among these ferns. And my eyes aren't lanterns either."

" Any way, François," said Madame Sévère half joking, half affectionately, " your eyes shine like glow-worms."

" So you can see them through the back of my hat ? " returned François, ruffled by what he took to be mockery.

" I can't see them now," said Madame Sévère with a sigh as heavy as herself, " but I have often seen them at other times ! "

" They have never had anything to tell you," responded the waif innocently. " You might leave them alone, for they have never offended you and never will either."

.   .   .   .   .

[" I fancy," remarked the curé's servant at this point, " that you can skip the next bit. It isn't very interesting to hear of all this bad woman's wicked attempts to upset our waif's religious notions."

" Don't worry, Mother Monique," answered the hemp-dresser ; " I will miss out anything unnecessary. I am aware I am speaking before young folk, and I won't say a word too many.

" We had got to where Madame Sévère was anxious to bring a less innocent look into François eyes than that he boasted about."]

" How old are you now, François ? " she asked him with politeness, so as to show him she did not want to treat him like a youngster.

" Oh gracious ! I don't know exactly," replied the waif, who began to see through her little games. " I don't often bother to count up my days ! "

" They say you are only seventeen," she went on, " but I bet you are twenty, for you are tall, and you will soon be having a beard."

" I don't care either way," yawned François.

" Hallo ! you're going too fast, my lad. I've lost my purse now."

" The deuce you have," snapped François, who had not realised the full extent of her cunning. " I suppose you will have to get down and look for it— probably it is valuable."

He jumped down and helped her to dismount ; she took the opportunity of leaning on him and he found her heavier than one of his sacks of corn.

She pretended to hunt for the purse which was in her pocket, and he went on five or six paces leading the mare.

" Oh ! won't you help me to look ? " she cried.

" I must hold the mare," he answered, " because she is thinking of her colt and will run off if I leave go the bridle."

Madame Sévère looked about for her purse beneath the mare's feet close to François, and he jumped to the fact that she had lost nothing unless indeed her wits had gone astray.

"We hadn't got as far as here," he said, "when you shouted about your purse, so you won't be likely to find it hereabouts."

"You think it's a put-up job then, you sly rogue," she cried, trying to pull his ear; "for I believe you are a rogue."

But François drew back and would not fool with her.

"No, no," he said, "since you have discovered your bag let's be off, for I'd rather go to sleep than romp about."

"Well, then, we'll chat," said Madame Sévère when she was up behind him again. "They say that beguiles the tedium of the road."

"I don't need to be beguiled," replied the waif. "I'm not bored at all."

"That's the first nice thing you've said, François!"

"If it was complimentary it was said without intention for I don't know how to pay compliments."

Madame Sévère began to get furious; but she was not ready to resort to the truth. "This boy must be a perfect simpleton," she said to herself. "If I made him lose his way he would have to stop with me a while."

And she tried to misdirect him, and to guide him to the left when he wanted to go to the right.

"You're straying," she told him; "it's the first time you've been this way—I know it better than you. Listen to me or you'll make me spend the night in the woods, young man."

But when François had been over a road only once he remembered it so well that he could have found his way a year later.

" No, no," he replied, " this is the way. I'm not cracked. The mare knows the road very well too, and I don't want to spend the night rambling about in the woods."

So it was they reached Dollins, the place where Madame Sévère lived, having wasted less than a quarter of an hour. And François had taken absolutely no heed of the woman's cajoleries.

When they arrived she tried to keep him on the pretext that the night was too dark, that the floods were out, and the fords swollen. But the waif cared not a jot for such dangers, and, bored with such senseless chatter, tightened his stirrups, set his horse at a gallop without listening to another word, and raced back to the mill where Madeleine awaited him, perturbed by the delay.

THE waif told Madeline nothing of what Madame Sévère had given him to understand. He dared not ; indeed he dared not even think about it. I don't say I would have been so prudent as he in such circumstances ; but, any way, prudence doesn't do any harm, and I only tell you what actually happened. This lad was as well-behaved as an innocent girl.

But thinking it over that night Madame Sévère felt offended with him and told herself he was probably more contemptuous than foolish. This idea set her brain afire and made her blood boil ; thoughts of revenge surged into her mind.

She planned to such effect that when Cadet Blanchet returned only partly sobered she gave him to understand that his assistant was an insolent young whippersnapper. She said she had to slap his face to keep him in check, for he had taken it into his head to make love to her and kiss her as they returned by night through the woods.

This was more than enough to upset Blanchet ; but she was not yet content, and jeered at him for leaving a likely lad of captivating manners in the house with his wife. Blanchet became jealous at once of his mistress and of his wife. He took his stick, jammed his hat down over his eyes like an extinguisher over a candle, and dashed off to the mill without pausing for breath.

Luckily the waif was out. Blanchet had bought a tree from Blanchard of Guerin which the waif had to fell and cut up into logs : he would not be home before evening. Blanchet would have gone after him at his work save that he feared if he showed any spite the young millers of Guerin would make a laughing-stock of him and his jealousy which hardly seemed to fit in with his ill-treatment and neglect of his wife. He would have waited in for him, but that being at home bored him. The quarrel he wanted to pick with his wife could not hold out all day ; you can't go on being angry when the ill-temper is all on your side. However, he could have got over the mockery and endured the boredom for the pleasure of giving the poor waif a sound drubbing, had not his walk sobered him somewhat and brought him to the realisation that the waif was no longer a child ; and a young man old enough to fall in love is old enough to use his fists in self-defence.

These considerations induced him to try to pull himself together, as he drank his pint in silence, and revolved in his head a tirade against his wife, unable to decide how to begin.

He said sourly as he came in that he wished to speak to her, and she waited in her usual attitude, sad, silent, and with a touch of proud reserve.

" Madame Blanchet," he said at last, " I want to give you an order which you wouldn't need if you were the woman you set up to be ! "

Therewith he stopped short as if to draw breath but actually because he was half ashamed of what he was about to say, for innocence was as clearly inscribed on his wife's face as a prayer in a Book of Hours.

Madeleine did not help him out at all. She made no sign, awaiting the end of his speech, expecting a reproach for some item of expenditure, and never dreaming of his real complaint.

"You behave as if you didn't understand me, Madame Blanchet," went on the miller. "As a matter of fact my meaning is perfectly obvious. I intend to throw *that* out, and the sooner the better, for I've had altogether too much of it."

"Throw what ? " asked Madeleine, astounded.

"Throw *what !* You don't dare to say throw *whom ?* "

"Great heavens ! no. I don't know what you mean," she said. " Talk sense if you want me to understand you."

"You'll make me lose my temper," cried Cadet Blanchet, bellowing like a bull. " I tell you that waif is not wanted in my house. If he is still about to-morrow morning I'll turn him out by dint of using my fists—unless he prefers to get under my mill-wheel."

" What wicked words, and what evil ideas, Miller Blanchet ! " said Madeleine, in spite of herself growing as white as her cap. " You will end up by ruining your business if you send the lad away ; for you will never find anyone to do your job so well for so little pay. Besides, what has the poor boy done that you want to dismiss him so unkindly ? "

" He makes me look a fool, I tell you, my good dame ; and I won't be made the laughing-stock of the country-side. He has become the master in my house and he merits a good cudgelling for what he has done."

It took a little time for Madeleine to grasp her husband's meaning. She had not an idea of it, and brought him all the arguments she could think of against this caprice. But she might have saved herself the trouble; he only became the more enraged. Seeing that it would grieve her to lose her good retainer François, he grew jealous again and said such cruel things that she understood at last and began to weep for shame, hurt pride, and deep sorrow.

This aggravated matters still further; Blanchet swore that she must be in love with the product of the foundling hospital, that he blushed for her, and that if she did not turn the waif out without delay he would beat to him death and grind him to powder.

To which she replied, raising her voice more than usual, that he was the master and could dispense with whose services he pleased but that he had no right to insult an honest woman, and that she cried to God and His angels to witness an injustice too great and too heavy to bear. This led her, against her will, to reproach him for his own misconduct and confront him with the truth that those who live in glass houses have no right to throw stones.

This luckless speech of Madeleine's made Blanchet more furious still, for he saw that he was in the wrong. He threatened to stop her mouth with a blow of his fist and he would have done so had not Jeannie, drawn by the noise, thrown himself between them without knowing the cause of their quarrel. He was pale and upset at hearing such an uproar. Blanchet attempted to dismiss him and he wept, upon which his father called him badly brought up, a cry-baby, and a coward, and said his mother would make nothing of him. Then he got up truculently, slashing his cane and swearing that he would slay the waif.

Madeleine, seeing him in such a violent rage, flung herself before him so boldly that he was taken by surprise and did not resist her : she snatched the stick from his hand and threw it into the river. Then, without any of her habitual meekness, she said : " Nothing will be gained by following up your wicked impulse. When you lose your head you are liable to bring trouble upon yourself, and if you have no feeling for others, at least think of yourself and of the possible consequences of a wicked action. For some time, my good husband, you have led an evil life and you are fast heading to a bad end. I want to stop you, at any rate to-day, from committing a sin for which you would be punished both in this world and the next. You shall not kill anyone. You can go back to where you came from rather than seek to revenge an insult you have never received. Go away now— I give you a command in your own interests and for the first time in my life. You will have to listen to it, and you are bound to see that in so doing I don't lose the respect I owe you. I swear to you on my honour that the waif will not be here to-morrow and that you can come back without fear of meeting him."

So saying, Madeleine opened the house door for her husband, and Cadet Blanchet, utterly dumbfounded at this change in her demeanour, and, at bottom, pleased with this way out and Madeleine's submission, replaced his hat on his head, and without another word returned to Madame Sévère. To her and her friends he boasted of having thrashed his wife and the boy ; but, disbelieving him, Madame Sévère felt no particular pleasure.

When Madeleine Blanchet was left alone she sent

Jeannie out to the fields in charge of the flocks and the goat, and she herself went down to the mill-gate. There was a patch of ground there, islanded by rivulets from the mill-stream, and covered with tree trunks so overgrown with branches and fresh shoots as to form a thick screen. Madeleine often went there to pray, for no one disturbed her and she could hide among the tall weeds as a moor-hen hides in her nest of green twigs.

As soon as she reached this spot she knelt down to pray. Madeleine's prayers brought her much relief and comfort ; but now she could think of nothing save the poor waif she was bidden to dismiss, this child who loved her so much that he would surely die away from her. She could not pray, and felt desperate at the thought of losing her only support and parting from the child of her heart. She wept so long and so bitterly that it is a miracle she revived ; her sobs choked her, and she fell at last senseless on the ground and lay there over an hour. At nightfall, however, she tried to recover herself, and hearing Jeannie return, singing, with his flock, she got up and went home to prepare the supper. A little later she heard the oxen returning with Blanchet's oak-logs, and Jeannie rushed gladly out to greet his friend François, whom he had missed all day. Poor little Jeannie had been miserable at the sight of his father's furious gesture against his beloved mother, and in the fields he had wept over it, without knowing the cause of their quarrel. But a child's sorrow and the dew on the grass soon vanish and Jeannie thought no more about it. Taking François' hand and frisking about like a young rabbit, he led him in to Madeleine.

84

François noticed Madeleine's red eyes and pale face at once. " Heavens ! " he said to himself, " something bad has happened in the house," and he paled and trembled in sympathy, watching her and awaiting an explanation. But Madeleine made him sit down and gave him his supper without saying a word ; he could not swallow a mouthful. Jeannie ate and chattered alone, and felt quite comforted, for his mother kissed him from time to time and encouraged him to eat. When he was in bed, and while the servant tidied the room, Madeleine went out, signing to François to follow, She crossed the meadow and went to the fountain ; there, taking her courage in both hands, she said to him :

" My child, unhappiness has befallen us, and God wills that we should be severely chastised. See how miserable I am, and, if you love me, be brave, for if you don't help me I don't know what will become of me."

François little guessed the truth, although he supposed at once that it was something to do with Blanchet.

" What are you talking about ? " he asked Madeleine, kissing her hands as if she were indeed his mother. " How can you think I would fail to support and comfort you ? Am I not your servant for the rest of my life ? Am I not your child who will work for you, and who is strong enough to provide for your needs ? Leave Miller Blanchet out of the question, let him spend everything on himself if he wants to. I'll feed and clothe you, you and Jeannie. If necessary I'll leave you for a while. I'll go and hire myself out—but not far away, you may be sure ; I should see you each day and come over for the day on Sundays. I am strong enough now to work and earn the needful amount. You are so modest and require so little! Well, now, you won't have to deprive yourself for others so much and you will be better off. Come now, Madame Blanchet, my dear mother, calm yourself and don't cry, for if you cry I think I shall die of grief."

Madeleine, seeing that he did not guess the truth, and that she must enlighten him, commended her soul to God and sought to prepare herself for inflicting so much pain on the poor waif.

"FRANÇOIS, my son," she said, "that isn't it. My husband is not ruined yet as far as I know the state of his business, and if fear of want was all my trouble you would not find me so upset. People fit to work have no need to fear poverty. Since I must tell you why I am heartsick—it is that Miller Blanchet has set himself against you and will no longer have you in the house."

"Oh! it is that, is it?" said François, getting to his feet. "Well, then, let him kill me at once, for in any case I can't survive such a blow. Yes, let him end my days, for I have been in his way a long while and I know he wishes me dead. Tell me where he is. I want to find him and to say to him: 'Why do you wish to be rid of me? Perhaps I can overcome your wicked reasons—and if you are still determined, say so, so that—so that—I don't know what I am saying, Madeleine, honestly I don't know; I don't understand myself and I don't know what I'm doing. My heart is numbed and my head whirls; either I am about to die or to go crazy."

And the poor waif flung himself down and beat his head with his fists as he had done the day Mother Zabelle tried to take him back to the foundling hospital. Seeing this, courage returned to Madeleine. She took his hands, his arms, and shook him violently to force him to listen to her.

87

"If you have no more will and resignation than a child," she said to him, "you do not deserve the love I give you and you will make me ashamed of having brought you up as my son. Get up! You are a man, remember, and a man can't roll on the ground like that. Listen to me, François, and tell me if you love me enough to overcome your grief and not to see me for a little while. You see, my child, it is to ensure my peace, and for my honour, otherwise my husband will cause me shame and suffering. Thus, for very love of me you must leave me to-day, as I have kept you until now for love of you. Love is shown in different ways according to time and circumstance. You must leave me at once, for, to stop the miller from doing something wrong, I have given my word that you shall be gone by to-morrow morning. To-morrow is St. John's term and you must go and hire yourself out—not too near here either, for if we often saw each other it would increase Miller Blanchet's idea."

"But what *is* his idea, Madeleine? What is his complaint against me? How have I misbehaved myself? Does he still think you rob the house to help me? That's impossible, for I am now in the house. I don't eat more than I need and I never steal a pin. Perhaps he thinks I keep my wages and that it costs too much. Well! let me follow up my idea of going to talk to him and explain that since poor Mother Zabelle died I have taken not a farthing from you, or if you prefer that I don't tell him that—and indeed, if I did, he would want to force you to return all the wages which you gave away in charity—well, I shall make his proposition for next term: I will offer to work for him for nothing! In that way he can't complain of anything and he will let me stay near you."

"No, no, no, François," replied Madeleine quickly, "that won't do at all; and if you said that to him he would fall into a rage with you and me which would lead to some misfortune."

"But why, on earth?" asked François. "What's the matter with him? Is it only for the pleasure of making us unhappy that he invents these suspicions?"

"My dear child, don't ask me why he is against you; I can't tell you. I would feel too much ashamed of him, and it would be better for us all if you didn't try to guess it. All I can tell you is that it is fulfilling your duty towards me to go. You are grown up now and strong. You can get on without me; and besides, you will earn more elsewhere, for here you won't take anything from me. Every child leaves his mother and goes out to work—many go far away. You will do as the others do, and I will be as unhappy as other mothers, I will weep, I will think about you, pray for you morning and night. . . ."

"Yes, and you will take another servant who won't look after you nor safeguard your son and your property, who may even hate you if Miller Blanchet forbids him to listen to you, and who will repeat all your good deeds to him twisting them till they appear bad. You will be miserable, and I will no longer be there to defend and console you! Ah! you think I am without courage because I am unhappy? You imagine I think only of myself and you tell me that I shall benefit by being away! I don't think of myself in any of this. What do I care

89

if I gain or lose ? I don't care to know how I shall control my grief. I don't care if I live or die—it is as God wills, and I am indifferent since I can no longer live for you. What gives me pain and what I can't bear is, that I see you will have to suffer. You will be down-trodden now, they are only sending me away in order that they may do as they wish with you."

" If God allows it to be," said Madeleine, " we must suffer what we cannot prevent. One should not make things worse by fretting against them. You know how unhappy I am—do you think it would make me happier to know you were ill, sick of life, and refusing consolation ? Instead it would soothe me more to know that you are behaving well and keeping yourself healthy and courageous because you are fond of me."

This last good reason won the waif over ; he promised, on his knees as in confessional, to do his best to bear his trouble bravely.

" Well, then," he said, wiping his eyes, " I will go off early and I will say good-bye here, my dear mother Madeleine ! Good-bye for ever, perhaps, for you did not say that I might see you again and talk to you. If you think I ought not to have that happiness again don't say so or I shall lose the courage to live. Leave me the hope that I shall find you again one day at this clear fountain where for the first time I found you nearly eleven years ago. From that day to this I have had nothing but happiness. And I won't forget all the joy I owe to God and you. I'll remember it to help me from to-morrow onwards to take things as they come. I go broken-hearted and sick with grief thinking of the unhappy state I leave you in, and that in leaving you I rob you of your best friend ; but you tell me that if I don't try to be comforted you will be still more miserable. Therefore, I will console myself as best I can by thinking about you, and I value your friendship too much to wish to lose it by cowardice. Good-bye, Madame Blanchet, leave me alone here for a little ; I shall be better when I have wept my fill. If my tears fall in the fountain you will think of me every time you come to do your washing. I want to gather some mint to put among my linen for I am going soon to pack my things ; and every time I smell the mint I shall fancy I am here and that I see you. Good-bye, good-bye, my dear mother, I don't want to go back to the house. I could quite well kiss my Jeannie without waking him—but I haven't the courage. Kiss him for me, please, and so that he shan't weep for me, tell him to-morrow that I'll be back soon. Then he will forget me a bit while expecting me back ; and by and by you will talk to him of his poor François so that he won't entirely forget me. Give me your blessing, Madeleine, as you did on the day of my first communion. I need it that God's grace may be on me."

And the poor waif knelt down saying that if ever he had unwittingly offended her he asked her pardon.

Madeleine swore that she had nothing to forgive, and gave him her blessing, ardently wishing she could make it as powerful as a blessing from God.

" And now," said François, " now I am becoming a waif again and no one will love me any more—won't you kiss me as you kissed me—it was a special privilege —on the day of my first communion ? I shall need to remind myself of all that to be sure that in your heart you will continue to be a mother to me."

Madeleine kissed the child as she used to kiss him when he was little. Nevertheless, if anyone had seen it Miller Blanchet would have been considered just in his behaviour, and this good woman with no thoughts of evil would have been criticised, though the Virgin Mary saw no ill in her act.

[" Nor do I," said the curé's servant.

" And I still less," rejoined the hemp-dresser. And he went on :]

She went back to the house, but did not sleep a wink that night. She heard François come in to do up his bundle in the next room, and heard him go out at the peep of day. She did not move until he had gone a good way so that her courage should not fail her, and when she heard him crossing the little bridge she cautiously set the door ajar without letting herself be seen so that she might see him once more from afar. She watched him pause and glance at the river and the mill as if to say farewell to them. Then he went quickly on after plucking a poplar leaf, which he put in his hat as is the custom to show that one is seeking a place.

Miller Blanchet came home at midday. He said nothing until his wife remarked :

" Well, you must go and hire someone to help in the mill, for François has gone and so you are without a servant."

" That's enough, wife," replied Blanchet, " I'm going ; but I warn you not to count on a young one."

That was all the thanks she got for giving in, and so hurt was she that she could not help showing it.

" Cadet Blanchet," she said, " I obeyed your wishes ; I have sent away a good person for no reason, and—I don't hide it from you—against my will. I don't ask you to be grateful to me ; but, in my turn, I give you an order : it is that you don't insult me, for I have done nothing to deserve it."

She said this in a way that Blanchet was unused to, and it had its effect on him.

" Come, my dear," he said, holding out his hand to her, " let's make peace on this score and think no more about it. Perhaps I was a little hasty in my words ; but you know I had my reasons for mistrusting that waif. The devil sends these brats into the world, and he is always at their heels. When they are good in one way they are bad in another. Thus, though I daresay it will not be easy to find such a hard worker —the devil had whispered wantonness into his ear, and I know one woman who has cause to complain of this."

" That woman is not your wife," replied Madeleine, " and very likely she lied. Even if she spoke the truth you would have no reason for suspecting me."

" Do I suspect you ? " said Blanchet, shrugging his shoulders. " My grudge was against him, and now he is gone I'll think no more about it. If I said something you didn't like it was said in jest."

" Such jests are not to my taste," replied Madeleine, " keep them for those who appreciate them."

A T first Madeleine Blanchet bore her sorrow
fairly well. She learnt from her new servant,
who had met François at the hiring-fair, that the
waif had hired himself for eighteen crowns a year to
a farmer near Aigurande who owned a large mill and
a good deal of land. She was glad to hear he had found
a good situation, and did her best to return to her
usual occupations without regretting him too deeply.
But in spite of herself her sorrow was great, and she
was ill for a long while with a mild fever, the effects
of which were so gradual that no one noticed her
illness. François had been right in saying that his
absence robbed her of her best friend. She grew
weary of her loneliness and lack of people to talk to.
She petted her son Jeannie still more, and indeed he
was truly a nice lad, with no more harm in him than a
lamb.

But besides the fact that he was too young to understand all she could have told François, he did not look
after her or show her the attentions François had at
that age. Jeannie loved his mother, even more than
children usually do, for she was a far better mother
than most. But he was never astonished or moved
by her generosity as François was. He took it for
granted that she should love him and caress him so
faithfully. He took it as his due, and counted on it
as a right ; whereas the waif was grateful for the

smallest attention and showed his gratitude by his behaviour, his words and looks, his blushes and tears, so that with him Madeleine forgot that she had neither rest, nor love, nor comfort in her household. Her unhappiness returned when she was left alone to ponder all the troubles from which that friendship had shielded her. There was no longer anyone to read with her, to care for the poor with her, to pray as she did, and even to joke with her from time to time good-humouredly and innocently. Things she saw, things she did, no longer interested her, only reminding her of the time when she had had a gentle and friendly companion. Whether she went to the vineyard, the orchard, the mill, there was no corner she had not passed ten thousand times with that child hanging on to her skirts or that brave, eager servant at her side. It was as if she had lost a dear and promising son and, however much she loved the remaining one, part of her love went begging.

Her husband, seeing her unwell and pitying her sadness and weariness, feared that she might become really ill ; he did not want to lose her, for she looked after his affairs well and saved as much as he himself wasted. As Madame Sévère would not let him go to the mill, he realised that unless Madeleine had charge of that side of his affairs he would soon be ruined. Although reprimanding her from habit and complaining that she was not careful enough, he realised that no one else would serve him so well.

He set himself to find a companion to amuse and assist her, and it so happened that on the death of an uncle the care of his youngest sister, who had been

under his guardianship, now fell upon Blanchet. He
had thought of sending her to live with Madame
Sévère, but his other relatives shamed him out of
such a plan. Besides which, when Madame Sévère
saw a promising young beauty in her fifteenth year,
she was not in the least desirous of having the care of
her, and told Blanchet that she was afraid of the risks
attendant on the guardianship of so young a girl.
Blanchet, therefore, knowing it would be a profitable
affair to take charge of his sister—the uncle who
brought her up had left her money in his will—and not
caring to confide her to other relatives, brought her
to his mill and presented her to his wife as a sister and
a companion. He said she was to learn to work and to
help in the house, but that Madeleine was not to make
her tasks so disagreeable that she would seek to live
elsewhere.

Madeleine willingly agreed to this arrangement.
Mariette Blanchet took her fancy on account of the
beauty which was so distasteful to Madame Sévère.
She thought a lovely face to be a sure indication of a
charm of mind and good nature. She welcomed
the girl rather as a daughter who might perhaps replace poor François than as a sister.

Meanwhile poor François endured his ill-luck as
patiently as possible, considering it was about the
worst that could have befallen any man or child. It
was probably fortunate for him that he fell sick under
the strain, for it proved the kindness of his master's
family who kept him at home instead of sending him
to the hospital, and nursed him carefully. This miller
was very unlike Blanchet, and his daughter—a woman
of thirty not yet married—had a reputation of being

charitable and good-hearted. And these people realised that, in spite of the accident of his ill-health, the waif was a real treasure.

He was so sturdy and able-bodied that he recovered more quickly than another would have done, and even though he started work before he was fit he did not have a relapse.

His conscience urged him to make up for lost time and pay back the kindness of his masters, though for a couple of months he suffered from the effects of his illness ; and when he began work each morning he felt as dazed as if he had fallen from a housetop. But he gradually recovered and he never liked to mention the pain it cost him to set about work. They were soon so pleased with him that they entrusted him with various jobs above his province. Since he could read and write they made him keep accounts, which no one had been able to do before—to the detriment of the business at the mill.

He was well off in spite of his sorrow, and as he had wisely refrained from mentioning his origin no one derided him for being a waif. But neither kind treatment, nor his work, nor his illness could make him forget Madeleine, the dear old mill at Cormoner, his little Jeannie, or the cemetery where Mother Zabelle was buried. His heart was far away, and on Sundays he did nothing but brood and so found no repose after the weekly toil. He was so far from home —more than sixteen miles away—that he never received news of it. He thought at first that he would get used to this, but he was consumed with anxiety, and he discovered ways of obtaining information about Madeleine at least twice a year. He used to frequent fairs, looking out for an acquaintance from the old place, and when he met one he made inquiries about all his friends, beginning prudently with those he cared for least, and concluding with Madeleine who interested him most : thus he got news of her and her family.

But it's growing late, friends, and I'm yawning over my story. I'll tell you the rest to-morrow, if you like. Good night, everybody.

And the hemp-dresser went off to bed, while the farm-labourer lit his lantern and escorted Mother Monique back to the parsonage, for she was an old woman and could not see the way very well.

THE next day we again gathered at the farm, and the hemp-dresser resumed his tale :—

François stayed about three years in a fine mill called Haultchampault, Baschampault, or Fréchampault (for in those parts as in ours " champault " is a common name), near Villechiron in the Aigurande district. I have been round about there twice, and found it a lovely and fertile part. The country folk are more prosperous, better housed and well-dressed ; plenty of business is done, and though the soil is scantier the crops are better. But the ground there is rougher. It is cut up by rocks and cleft by streams. But it is pretty and charming there all the same. The trees are wondrously beautiful, and the two Creuses run babbling through their channels as clear as crystal springs.

The mills there are of more consequence than ours, and the one where François lived was among the largest and best. One winter's day, his master, whose name was Jean Vertaud, said to him :

" François, my friend and servant, I have a few words to say to you. Pray listen carefully. We have known each other some time, you and I, and I don't want to hide the fact that if more money has been coming in, if my mill is prosperous and I have done better than my neighbours, if—to cut a long story short—I have been able to increase my worldly goods, it is due to you. You have assisted me not as a servant, but as a friend and relative. You studied my interests as if they were your own. You managed my affairs as I should never be able to do, and throughout you have shown greater knowledge and understanding than I possess. I am over-credulous by nature, and I should have been perpetually cheated if you hadn't managed everybody and everything around me. Those who were in the habit of abusing my good nature grumbled, but you bore the brunt boldly, and in so doing exposed yourself more than once to dangers which you always overcame by your courage and kindness. What particularly pleases me is that you are as good-natured as you are willing and intelligent. You like scrupulousness but not avarice. You don't allow people to cheat you like me, and yet, like me, you are ready to give anyone a helping hand. You are the first to beg me to assist those actually in want. You have prevented rogues from deceiving me. And for a country fellow you are well-educated, you have brains and sense. Your ideas are always successful, and everything you put your hand to turns out well.

"I am very pleased with you, and I would gladly do you a good turn. Tell me frankly if there is anything you wish me to do for you—whatever it is I won't refuse."

"I don't know why you suggest that," answered François, "it seems to me you must think me discontented, and I assure you that is not so."

"I don't say you're discontented. But there is something in your expression and manner which shows you aren't really happy. You aren't at all gay, you never laugh, you never enjoy yourself. You are so quiet one would think you in mourning for someone."

"Are you annoyed with me for that, sir? In that respect I can't oblige you. I dislike drinking and dancing. I never go to inns or to parties; I don't know any songs or funny stories. Nothing which distracts me from work gives me any pleasure."

"Well, that is very admirable, my lad, and I would be the last to blame you for it. I mentioned it because I imagined you were in trouble of some kind. Perhaps you feel that you work extremely hard for others and that no benefit will come of it."

"You are wrong there, sir. I am as well rewarded as I could wish; nowhere else could I have earned the high wages you insist on paying me unasked. You have given me a rise each year and last St. John's term my wages reached a hundred crowns which makes it very dear for you. If you find it difficult to pay I will willingly accept less, I assure you."

"COME, come François, we are at cross purposes," replied Jean Vertaud, "and I don't know how to take you. You are by no means a fool and I thought I had given you a broad enough hint; but since you are so modest I must help you out. Isn't there any girl round here who takes your fancy?"

"No, sir," answered François unhesitatingly.

"Really?"

"I give you my word."

"If you had means isn't there one you'd care for at all?"

"I don't want to marry."

"What a notion! You're too young to know. But what's your reason?"

"Reason!" echoed François. "Are you interested in it, sir?"

"Yes, since I feel affection for you."

"I'll tell it you; there's no point in hiding it. I have never known father or mother . . . and, listen, here's a thing I've never mentioned; I wasn't forced to tell you, but had you asked me I wouldn't have lied to you. I am a waif. I come from a foundling hospital."

"Is that so?" exclaimed Jean Vertaud, rather taken aback by this confession. "I would never have thought it!"

"Why wouldn't you have thought it? . . . Why,

don't you reply, Master Vertaud ? Well, I'll answer the question for you. It is because seeing me well-behaved you would have been astonished that a waif could be so. Is it true, then, that waifs are suspected by everyone, and that there is something against them ? That is neither just nor humane ; however, there it is, and one has to put up with it, for the best-natured people feel the same, and even you . . ."

" No, no," said the miller, recovering himself, for he was an honourable man and was anxious to make up for a bad thought ; " I don't want to be unjust, and if I was forgetful of that for a second you can forgive me, for it is already over. You feel you can't marry, then, since you are a waif ? "

" It is not that, sir, and I am not worried about such a drawback. Women have all sorts of notions, and some are so good-hearted that that would be an additional reason."

" Well, I declare, you are quite right," said Jean Vertaud. " Women are worth more than we are ! . . . Besides," he added laughing, " a handsome lad like you, glowing with youth, whole in mind and body, might well add zest to the exercise of benevolence ! But let's hear your reason."

" Listen," said François. " A woman I never knew took me from the foundling hospital and nursed me. When she died, another woman took charge of me for the sake of the small amount of money allowed by the government to me and my like ; but she was kind to me, and when I had the misfortune to lose her I would have been inconsolable but for the care of a woman who was the kindest of the three, and for whom I have so great a love that I want to live for no one but her. However, I've left her and shall perhaps never see her again, for she is well-off and may never have need of me. But very likely her husband, who, I am told, has been ill since the autumn, and who has run up debts no one knows of, may die soon and leave her with more creditors than property. If that happens, I tell you openly, sir, I shall go back to her. I will undertake no other task than that of helping her and her son, and by working for her ward off the burden of want. That is why I have no wish to bind myself in any other direction. I am working for you by the year, but when I marry I am bound for my whole life. Besides, it would be too heavy a load on my shoulders. When I had a wife and child how would I manage to support two households? And beyond that, even if the impossible happened and I found a wife with a little property, would I have the right to take from my own house and give to another? Therefore I prefer to remain unmarried. I am young, and so far my time has not come; still, even if some love affair came my way I would do my best to dismiss it, for, mark you, there is only one woman for me and that is my mother Madeleine, she who never despised me for being a waif, and who brought me up as if I were her own son."

"Well, my friend, what you have just told me increases my respect for you," replied Jean Vertaud. "There is nothing so hideous as ingratitude, nothing so charming as acknowledgment of benefits received. There are good reasons I could give you to show you could marry a young woman with the same ideas as yourself and who would help you to assist the old lady;

but I'll have to consult someone about those reasons first."

No particular cleverness is needed to see that out of goodness of heart and shrewdness of judgment Jean Vertaud had planned a marriage between his daughter and François. She was not at all bad-looking, and if she was a little older she had money enough to equalise the difference. She was an only girl and a good match; but up to the present she had not wanted to marry, to her father's disappointment. When he noticed that she seemed to make much of François he had questioned her on the subject; as she was a very reserved young woman he had been unable to draw her out; but at last, without giving a positive reply, she had consented to allow her father to sound François on the subject of marriage, and she was awaiting results with more anxiety than she would have had him know.

Jean Vertaud would have liked to be able to give her a more definite answer; firstly because he wanted to see her settled in life, and secondly because he could not hope for a better son-in-law than François. In addition to his affection for the lad he saw that, despite his poverty on arrival, he was worth a good deal in a family for his intelligence, quick work, and good behaviour.

The fact that François was a waif upset the miller's daughter, for she was rather proud; but she soon decided in his favour, and her eagerness increased on hearing that François was backward in loving. Women go by contraries, and if François had plotted to overcome the drawback of his birth he could not have done it in a better way than by showing a distaste for marriage. Thus from that day Jean Vertaud's daughter set her heart more earnestly on winning François.

"Is that all it is ? " she said to her father. "He thinks we would have neither the will nor the means to assist an old woman and to find a situation for her boy ? He couldn't have understood your hints, father, for had he known it was a matter of entering our family he would not have worried on that account."

And that evening, between supper and bedtime, Jeannette Vertaud said to François : "I had a very high opinion of you, François, but you have gone up still more in my estimation since my father told me of your affection for the woman who brought you up and for whom you want to work all your life. It is your duty to feel so on this matter. . . . I would love to know the woman for whom you have retained so great an attachment so that I could help her if need be ; she must be a nice woman."

"Oh yes," said François, only too pleased to talk about Madeleine, "she is a thoughtful woman with the same ideas as yourselves."

These words rejoiced Jean Vertaud's daughter, and, sure of herself, she added :

"I hope that if she met with misfortune as you fear she may, she would come to stay with us. I would help you to look after her, for I suppose she is no longer young ? Is she not an invalid ? "

"An invalid ? No," said François, "she is not old enough to be infirm."

"Is she still young then ? " asked Jeannette Vertaud, beginning to prick up her ears.

"Oh no, not at all," replied François simply. "I

don't remember how old she would be by now. She was like a mother to me, and I never troubled about her age."

"Was she a fine woman?" demanded Jeannette after a moment's hesitation.

"Fine?" said François a little surprised. "Do you mean is she a pretty woman? For me she is pretty enough as she is; but, as a matter of fact, I have never thought about it. What difference could it make to my affection? She might be uglier than the devil and I should never have noticed it."

"Yes, but you can say round about how old she is?"

"Wait a minute! her son is five years younger than I am. Well, she's not old but she's not very young either: she's about like . . ."

"Like me?" said Jeannette, forcing a laugh. "In that case if she became a widow she would be too old to marry again, wouldn't she?"

"It depends," replied François. "If her husband doesn't waste everything but leaves her a little property she won't lack suitors. There are fellows who, for money's sake, would as soon marry their grand-aunts as their grand-nieces."

"And you don't admire people who marry for money?"

"I wouldn't care about it," replied François. The waif, though simple-hearted, was not so simple-minded that he had not in the end understood her insinuations. His last remark was made with intention. But Jeannette ignored it and fell more deeply in love with him. She had been much courted without caring for any of her suitors. The first who attracted her was he who turned his back on her—so reasonable are women !

François noticed in the next few days that she was troubled, that she ate practically nothing, and that when he appeared to be looking the other way she fixed her eyes on him. Her caprice worried him. He respected this good young woman and he saw clearly that indifference on his part made her the more in love. But he did not care for her, and had he taken her it would have been calculatingly and out of duty rather than for real love.

He saw that he had better leave Jean Vertaud's employ for, sooner or later, this business would lead to trouble or annoyance. But just at this time something happened which altered all his plans.

ONE morning the curé of Aigurande came as if for a walk to Jean Vertaud's mill. He patrolled up and down for a while until he could buttonhole François in a corner of the garden. He assumed a very confidential manner and asked him if he was really François called Strawberry, a name which he had been given (because of a birthmark on his left arm) by the officials to whom he had been delivered as a waif. The curé also asked his age as nearly as possible, the name of the women who had nursed him, where he had lived ; in short, all he could tell him of his birth and his life.

François went to consult his papers and the curé seemed quite satisfied.

" Well," he said to him, " come to the parsonage to-morrow, or this evening, and don't tell anyone what I shall have to let you know, for I am forbidden to spread the story, and it is a matter of conscience."

When François arrived at the parsonage, the curé shut the doors, and drew from his cupboard four bits of thin paper, saying, " François Strawberry, there are four thousand francs sent by your mother. I am forbidden to tell you her name, or in what part of the country she lives, or if she is alive or dead now. A religious thought has caused her to remember you, and it appears she has always intended to do so, for she knew how to find you though living far away.

She knows you are a good lad, and she sends you the means of setting up for yourself on condition that you don't speak of this gift for six months unless it be to the woman you wish to marry. She asked me to consult you about its use or deposit, and also she asked me to let you use my name so as to keep the thing secret. I will do what you like about it ; but I am instructed only to allow you the money on your word not to say anything or do anything which might disclose the secret. I know I can rely on your word ; will you give it me ? "

François agreed and left the money in the curé's hands, asking him to deal with it as he thought fit ; for he knew the priest to be a good man and they, like women-folk, are all virtue or all vice.

The waif returned to the house more sad than joyful. He thought of his mother ; he would have given the four thousand francs to see her and kiss her. But he told himself that very likely she had just died, and the money came to him under her will ; this made him still sadder to be deprived of wearing mourning and saying masses for her. He prayed God to pardon her, alive or dead, for abandoning her child, as her child pardoned her, and he asked forgiveness also for his own sins.

He tried not to show signs of worry, but for a couple of weeks he was absorbed in reveries at meal times to the astonishment of the Vertauds.

"The lad isn't being open with us," observed the miller. "He must be in love."

"Perhaps with me," thought his daughter, "and he refrains from confessing it out of delicacy. He fears people will say he cares more for my wealth than for me. And he behaves like this to hide his grief."

Thereupon she decided to cajole his shyness, and encouraged him so charmingly with looks and words that he was a little roused from his depression.

At times he said to himself that since he was rich enough to aid Madeleine if need be, he could very well marry a girl who would not want his money. He was not in love with anyone ; but he was aware of Jeannette Vertaud's good qualities and he was afraid of seeming unkind in taking no notice of her advances. Sometimes his pity overcame him so that he half thought of consoling her. But suddenly, during a journey to Crevant on his master's business, he met a roadman who lived near Presles and who told him of Cadet Blanchet's death, adding that he had left his affairs in a muddle and it was not known if his widow would be well or badly off.

François had no reason for liking or regretting Miller Blanchet. Yet he was so tender-hearted that tears stung his eyes and he felt like weeping when he heard this news ; he thought that Madeleine would be lamenting her husband at that time, pardoning all and remembering nothing save that he was the father of her child. And Madeleine's grief found an answer in his own heart and caused him to weep too for the sorrow she must be enduring. He longed to jump on his horse and go to her ; but he felt it his duty to ask his master's permission first.

"SIR," said he to Jean Vertaud, "I have to go away for a time—I don't know if it will be long or short. I have some business to do near my old place, and I wonder if you will let me go in a friendly spirit ; though, to speak plainly, if you are unwilling to grant permission I can't oblige you, for go I must in any case. Pardon me for being so outspoken. I should be sorry to cause you annoyance, and so I ask you as the only thanks for any service I have been able to render not to take it amiss that I leave you now. It is probable that I shall be back in a week if they don't need me where I am going. But it is equally likely that I shan't come back until late in the year or not at all—for I don't want to mislead you. However, I would return at any time if it lay in my power to lend you a hand with anything you couldn't manage without my help. And before I leave I want to find a good worker to replace me and to whom—if it is necessary in order to persuade him to come to you— I will give up the wages due to me at last St. John's term. In that way we can arrange things without much bother for you ; and you might shake hands with me to cheer me up a little on leaving you and to bring me luck."

Jean Vertaud knew that the waif was not often set on having his own way, but that when he was, neither God nor the devil could turn him from his purpose.

"You can be quite happy about it, my boy," said he, shaking hands; "it would be a lie to say it makes no difference to me. But rather than have a tiff with you I'd agree to anything."

François spent the next day in seeking a successor for the mill, and he found a good reliable man just out of the army and pleased to find well-paid work under a kind master—for Jean Vertaud had that reputation and had never wronged a soul.

Before leaving, as he intended to do at dawn the following day, François wanted to say good-bye to Jeannette Vertaud at supper time. She was sitting on the step of the barn, saying she had a headache and wanted nothing to eat. He realised that she had been weeping and this disturbed him. He did not know how to begin to thank her for her goodness and to tell her he must go in spite of it. He sat down on an alder stump near her seat and strove to speak, but was unable to utter a single word. Thereupon she, knowing him to be there without looking up, put her handkerchief to her eyes. He raised his hand to take hers comfortingly but it occurred to him that he could not truthfully tell her what she wanted to hear. And when poor Jeannette saw that he did not move she felt ashamed of her grief, and, rising quietly and without any show of temper, she went into the barn to weep her fill. She lingered there a while thinking he would perhaps follow her and say something nice, but he went in to supper without allowing himself to go to her and ate his meal sadly and in silence.

It would be untrue to say that he did not feel for her on seeing her tears. His heart was touched and he felt he could have been quite happy with such a nice woman so fond of him and whom he found it pleasant to caresss. But he dismissed these ideas, thinking that Madeleine might need a friend, a counsellor, and a helper. And she had suffered and worked and been abused for his sake when he was a miserable homeless child sick with fevers.

"Now then," said he to himself next morning as he got up before daybreak, "no love affairs or fortune or peace for you! You are willing to forget you are a waif and to put aside the past like dozens of others who enjoy the present without looking back; but Madeleine Blanchet is in your heart and she says "Take care you don't forget what I did for you." Let me be off then, and may God help you, Jeannette, to find a nicer lover than your servant."

As he was thinking this he passed his good mistress's window, and had it been possible he would have left a flower or a leaf by the pane as a token of farewell; but it was the day after Twelfth Night; the earth was snow covered, there were no leaves on the trees, and not even a violet in the grass. So he knotted the favour he had won as king of Twelfth night at the celebrations the evening before in the corner of a white handkerchief and tied it to Jeannette's window-bar to show her he would have chosen her as his queen had she been present at supper.

"It isn't anything much," he said to himself, "but it is a token of goodwill and friendship which will absolve me from saying good-bye."

But he seemed to hear a voice within him dissuading him from leaving his gift and saying that a man has no right to behave like these young women who want to be loved, thought upon, and regretted, when they themselves have no corresponding feelings.

" No, no, François," said he, putting his favour back into his pocket and hastening his steps : " one must remain fixed on one's purpose and make others forget when one has resolved to forget them."

And thereupon he set off at a great rate, and before he had gone a couple of gunshots' distance from Jean Vertaud's mill he fancied he saw Madeleine and imagined he heard a feeble cry for help. He seemed to see the apple-tree, the fountain, Blanchet's meadow, the dam, the little bridge, and Jeannie rushing to meet him ; the thought of Jeannette Vertaud was not strong enough to hold him back from all this. He went so fast that he did not feel the cold, he did not think of food or drink, nor did he pause until he had left the main road and reached by way of the short cut to Presles the wooden cross of Plessys.

There he knelt and fervently kissed the wood as a good Christian who recovers a friend. After that he went on down the hill ; the way here is as wide as a field, it is the finest pasture in the world, high up, open to the four winds and the sky, and so steep in descent that when it is frozen over even an ox-waggon would slide rapidly down and might fall headlong into the river which runs unseen below it.

François mistrusted it and took off his sabots more than once ; he reached the footbridge without mishap. Leaving Montipouret on his left, he gave a gay good-day to the solid old belfry beloved of everybody, for it is the first sight the wanderer has of home and is a guide to those who have lost their way.

I don't mind the roads at all, they are so smiling, green, and pleasant to see in the warm sun. There are shady roads where the sun does not beat fiercely on one's head. But they are the most treacherous, for you might easily follow them to Rome imagining you are on the way to Angibault. Luckily the old belfry of Montipouret rears itself gallantly, and its gleaming point strikes through the rifts to show you whether your face is set to eastward or to westward.

But the waif had no need of such beacons to guide him. He knew every twist and turn of the road, all the byways and highways, all the tracks and paths, the very hedges, so that he could have taken the shortest way, as a crow flies, even at the dead of night.

About midday he perceived the roof of the mill at Cormouer through the leafless trees, and he was glad to see by the thread of blue smoke uprising from its chimneys that the dwelling had not been abandoned to the rats.

He cut across Blanchet's meadow and thus missed passing the fountain, but he saw through the bare boughs and bushes the sun glinting on the water which never freezes for it comes from the spring. The approach to the mill was frozen, however, and so slippery that even a nimble person might have tripped on the stones and the river banks. He saw the old mill-wheel, black with age and damp, with long icicles as sharp as needles hanging from its sails. But many trees were missing from around the mill and the place wore a changed look. Blanchet's debts had set the axe to work after his death, and in many places the fresh-cut alder stumps showed red as martyrs' blood. The house had a derelict air, the roof needed repair, and the furnace was partly corroded by the frost.

Then, sadder still, there was no sound about the place, no human being, no animal, nothing ; save that a dog with a grey coat with black and white patches— one of the miserable country mongrels—came out of the doorway and shambled, yelping, to meet the waif ; he ceased barking at once, however, and lay down at François' feet.

" Well, well, Labriche, so you know me ? " François said to him.   " I wouldn't have recognised you, so old, so skinny, that your ribs stick out, and with white whiskers ! "

François rambled on thus as he looked at the dog, for he was quite overcome and seemed to want to gain time before entering the house.   Up till then he had been in a vast hurry, but now he was afraid, imagining he might never see Madeleine again, that she had gone away, or that she, and not the miller, had died, or that he had been misled by false news of his death ; in short, François experienced all the emotions of one within reach of his heart's desire.

A T last he lifted the latch of the door and there
stood before him not Madeleine, but a pretty
well-built young woman, as rosy as a dawn in Spring
and as lively as a cricket.

"What do you want, young man?" she asked
pleasantly.

Charming as was her appearance François did not
keep his eyes on her long but looked round the room
for the miller's widow. All he saw was that her bed-
curtains were drawn; she was doubtless in bed.
He never thought of replying to the pretty girl who
was the younger sister of the dead miller and whose
name was Mariette Blanchet. He went straight to
the yellow bed and, without argument or question,
cautiously drew back the curtain; there he saw
Madeleine Blanchet stretched out, pale, unconscious,
and wasted with fever. He watched and examined
her for a long time without moving or speaking: and
despite his grief at finding her ill, despite his fear that
she might die, he was overjoyed to see her face again
and to say to himself:

"I am looking on Madeleine."

But Mariette Blanchet pushed him gently away
from the bed, drew the curtain, and beckoned to
him to go over to the hearth with her.

"And now, young sir," she said, "who are you,
and what do you want? I don't know you, and

you are not of these parts. What can I do for you ? "

But François did not hear her, and instead of replying asked her how long Madame Blanchet had been ill, if her life was in danger, and if she was being properly nursed.

To which Mariette replied that she had been ill since her husband's death, because of the strain of nursing and tending him day and night ; that the doctor had not been sent for but that if she grew worse someone would go for him ; and as for being nursed properly she, Mariette, did not spare herself as was her duty.

At these words the waif looked at her attentively and there was no need for him to ask her name, for, besides knowing that about the time he himself left them Blanchet had taken his sister into his house, he recognised in the pretty face of that sweet young girl a marked resemblance to the unpleasant face of the dead miller. There are many attractive faces which resemble ugly ones though it is difficult to say how that may be. And though Mariette Blanchet was as sweet a sight as her brother had been unpleasing there was an unmistakable family likeness. However, where the miller's expression had been morose and sullen Mariette looked more of a tease than irritable and more fearless than fearsome.

Now François did not feel entirely comfortable about her ability to assist Madeleine though he was not very troubled about it either.

Her cap was white, well-laundered and well-set, her hair, done rather in the fashion of a townswoman, was shining, cared for, and neatly dressed ; her hands were white and her apron also for a sick nurse. In short, she was extremely young, smart, and irresponsible to be thinking day and night of a person too far gone to help herself at all.

This reflection decided François to seat himself in the chimney-corner without further question and not to leave the place until he saw if his dear Madeleine was on the road to recovery or if her illness was fatal.

Mariette was much astonished to see him unceremoniously take possession of the fire and make himself at home. He bent over the embers and appeared so unwilling to chat that she did not dare seek again to know who he was or what he wanted.

But a moment later in came Catherine, for eighteen or twenty years servant in the house ; and without noticing him she went to her mistress's bed, glanced warily at her, and then crossed to the fireplace to see how Mariette was getting on with the invalid's drink she was preparing. Her whole bearing manifested great solicitude for Madeleine, and François, feeling her sincerity, in a *jerk*, longed to say a friendly goodday ; but . . .

.   .   .   .   .

" But," said the curé's servant, interrupting the hemp-dresser " you used an unreasonable word. ' Jerk ' doesn't mean a moment or a minute either."

" Well, I tell you," replied the hemp-dresser, " a moment doesn't mean anything and an idea passes through one's brain in less than a minute. I don't know how many things you can think of in a minute. Now, to see and understand a thing happening takes only the time of a ' jerk.' I'll call it a ' tiny jerk ' if you like."

" But a ' jerk ' of time ! " objected the old purist.

" Ah ! a ' jerk ' of time ! That upsets you, Mother Monique ? Doesn't everything work by ' jerks ' like that. The sun rising in flaming leaps, and your eyes blinking as you look at it, the blood throbbing in the veins, the church-clock dropping the time crumb by crumb as the sifter drops the wheaten grain, your rosary as you tell it, your heart when the curé is late home, the rain falling drop by drop, and even, we are told, the earth turning like a mill-wheel ? You don't feel it going—nor do I ; the machine is too well oiled ; but the ' jerks ' must go on for we revolve round so far in twenty-four hours. And we also use ' round ' to indicate a certain time. Then I can say ' jerk '—and I won't retract it. And don't interrupt me if you want me to go on."

" No, no—your machine is also too well oiled," replied the old woman. " Give your tongue another of your ' jerks ' then."

I WAS saying that François was tempted to greet old Catherine and make himself known to her; but as, in the same 'jerk' of time, he felt like weeping, he was ashamed of looking a fool, and did not even raise his head. But as she bent over the fireplace Catherine saw his long legs and drew back in alarm.

"Whoever is that?" she whispered to Mariette in a corner of the room. "Where has this chap come from?"

"Don't ask me," replied the girl, "how should I know! I've never seen him before. He came in unceremoniously as if to an inn without saying a word of greeting. He asked about my sister-in-law as if he were a relative or one of the heirs; and there he is sitting by the fire as you see. Speak to him yourself, I don't want to. Perhaps he is not quite all there."

"What! you think he is out of his mind? All the same he doesn't look wicked as far as I can see for he seems to be trying to hide his face."

"Suppose he is up to no good?"

"Don't be afraid, Mariette, I'm here to stop him. If he interferes with us I will throw a pan of boiling water over his legs and the fire-irons at his head."

While they were chattering thus François was thinking of Madeleine.

" Poor thing," he was thinking, " she, who has never had anything but misery and bad treatment from her husband, is lying ill there because she took care of him and nursed him until the hour of his death. And here is this young girl, his sister—and spoiled by him from all accounts—she doesn't show much anxiety in her features. If she is tired and has been crying she doesn't show it, her eyes are as clear and bright as the sun."

He could not help watching her from beneath his hat, for he had never seen so fresh and sprightly a beauty. But though her appearance fascinated him it went no deeper.

" Come along now," Catherine continued whispering to her young mistress, " I'm going to speak to him. We must find out what he intends to do."

" Speak nicely," said Mariette, " we don't want to upset him ; we are alone in the house. Jeannie is probably a good way away and would not hear us call out."

" Jeannie ! " echoed François, who had caught the name of his old friend amongst all this whispering. " Where is Jeannie that I can't see him ? Is he tall, is he handsome, and strong ? "

" Dear me ! " thought Catherine, " he asks that because he has bad intentions very likely. Now, who in heaven's name can he be ? I don't know him by his figure or by his voice ; I'll know the rights of it and have a look at his face."

She would not have shrunk from confronting the devil himself, for she was as stoutly built as a plough-man and as bold as a soldier, so she stepped up to him determined to make him take off his hat, or to knock it off to see if he was a ruffian or a decent fellow. She went for the waif, never dreaming that it could be François. His mood was such that he never noticed her, and she on her part had forgotten him long since ; besides, he had so much improved that she would have had to look more than once to recognise him. But as she went up to give him a poke and possibly to insult him, Madeleine roused and called to Catherine so feebly that her voice was almost inaudible, saying she was burning with thirst.

François jumped up and would have been first at her side but he feared to give her a shock. He contented himself with giving Catherine the drink as quickly as possible, and she, taking it, hurried to her mistress, forgetting for the moment to bother about anything but her condition. Mariette also took her share by lifting Madeleine in her arms to give her a drink, and it was not hard, for Madeleine had become pitifully thin and wasted.

" How do you feel, my dear sister ? " asked Mariette.

" Quite well, quite well, my child," replied Madeleine in the voice of a dying person ; she never complained, so as to prevent others from worrying.

" But," she said, looking at the waif, " that isn't Jeannie over there ? Who is it, my child, if I am not dreaming, that tall man by the fireplace ? "

And Catherine answered :

" We don't know, ma'am ; he doesn't speak, he stands there like a half-wit."

The waif made a slight movement as he looked at Madeleine, afraid to go to her too soon and yet dying to speak. Catherine saw his face then ; but she did not know him after three years, and, thinking Madeleine afraid, replied, "Don't you worry, ma'am; I was about to get rid of him as you called me."

"Don't send him away," Madeleine said in a slightly stronger voice, and drawing her curtain further back, "I know him, and he has done well to come to see me. Come here, come here, my son; every day I have prayed to God to let me give you my blessing."

And the waif ran and flung himself on his knees by her bed, sobbing for grief and joy until he nearly choked. Madeleine held his hands and then his head, and kissed him saying:

"Call Jeannie: Catherine, call Jeannie so that he may rejoice too. Oh! I thank God, François; and now I can die if it is His will, for both my children are grown-up and I can bid them farewell."

CATHERINE hurried out to fetch Jeannie, followed by Mariette eager to find out what all this might mean.

François was left alone with Madeleine who kissed him again and began to cry : presently she closed her eyes and fell into an even worse state than before. François did not know how to revive her from her swoon : he was quite demented, and could only hold her in his arms calling her his dear mother, his dear friend, and beseeching her, as if it lay in her power, not to leave this life so quickly and without hearing what he had to tell her.

So, with anxious words, tender care, and gentle caresses he brought her back to consciousness. She began to recognise him and to listen to him. And he told her how he had guessed her need of him and had left everything to get to her; he said he would not leave her again as long as she asked him to stay, and that if she wanted him for her servant he asked nothing more than the pleasure of waiting on her and the delight of spending his days obedient to her will. And he added :

"Don't answer, don't speak, my dear mother, you are too weak, don't say anything. Only look at me if you are glad to see me and I will know that you want my friendship and my service."

Madeleine looked at him contentedly and listened,

comforted, and they were happy together in spite of the sorrow of her illness.

Jeannie, summoned by Catherine's lusty shouts, came in to share their joy. He had grown into a handsome boy between fourteen and fifteen years of age, not very strong, but pleasingly alert, and so well brought up that he always spoke nicely and in a friendly way.

"Oh, I'm glad to see you like this, Jeannie," François said to him. "You're not very tall or stout, but I'm glad of that, for I fancy you'll still need my help to climb trees or ford the river. You are still a little delicate without being ill, aren't you? Oh well, you can be my child a bit longer if you like; yes, yes, you still need me; and you will make me obey your whims as in the old days."

"Yes, my four hundred whims, as you used to say," said Jeannie.

"My word, yes! What a memory he has! Ah! it is dear of you, Jeannie, not to have forgotten your François. And have we still our four hundred whims a day?"

"Oh, no," said Madeleine, "he is very sensible now, he has only about two hundred."

"Neither more nor less?"

"Oh! I don't mind," replied Jeannie; "since my darling mother is beginning to laugh again, I'll agree with whatever anyone likes. And I must say that just now I have the whim more than five hundred times a day of wanting to see her cured."

"Well said, Jeannie," said François. "See how well the child has learnt to talk! Listen, my boy, God will satisfy your five hundred whims on that score. We are going to look after your darling mother and cheer her up, and little by little make her laugh so that her sickness will go away."

Catherine was on the doorstep, anxious to come in to see and talk to François, but Mariette held her arm and never stopped questioning her.

" What ! " she said, " a waif ! He looks very decent, anyway."

And she peered through the crack in the door which she held ajar.

" But how is it he is so friendly with Madeleine ? "

" Didn't I tell you she brought him up, and he was a very good fellow too."

" Yes, but she never mentioned him to me, nor did you either."

" Oh Lord, I never thought about it ; he had gone away and I had almost forgotten him ; besides I knew that our mistress had been in trouble on his account and I didn't want to rake up the past."

" In trouble ? How in trouble ? "

" Lord ! because she was so fond of him ; she could not help it, he was so good-natured, that child, and your brother wouldn't have him in the house ; your brother isn't always very nice as you know ! "

" We mustn't say that now he is dead, Catherine."

" Yes, yes, you're right. I had forgotten, I declare ; my memory's so bad. And yet—it is only a fortnight ago. But let me go in, miss ; I want to give the boy a meal. I expect he is hungry." And she pulled her arm away and went up to kiss François ; he was such a handsome lad that she quite forgot her bygone remark that she would sooner kiss her sabot than a waif.

" Well, my dear François," she said to him, " how glad I am to see you ! I thought you were never coming back. But just look, madame, how he has grown up ! I am surprised you knew him at once. If you hadn't said who it was it would have taken me some time to recognise him. Isn't he handsome ? isn't he ? And he's beginning to have a beard ! It doesn't show much, but you can feel it. Lord ! when you left, François, that couldn't be felt—now it does just prick one. And what a strong thing he is, my dear ! What arms, what hands, and such legs too ! A workman like that is worth three ordinary men. How much do they pay you over there ? "

Madeleine laughed softly to see how pleased Catherine was with François, and she watched him, equally glad to have him back in his glowing youth and health. She would have liked to see Jeannie grow up into such a fine young man. As for Mariette she was shocked to see Catherine so boldly admiring a youth, and she had grown scarlet—though quite innocently. But the more she tried to refrain from looking at François the more her eyes strayed towards him and she perceived him to be, as Catherine had said, wonderfully good-looking and as sturdy as an oak sapling.

And then, without stopping to think, she began to wait on him nicely, to pour out the best wine of the year's vintage and to rouse him when, watching Madeleine and Jeannie, he forgot to eat.

" Come, eat more than that," she said to him, " you have hardly touched a thing. You ought to have more appetite since you have come such a long way ! "

" Don't take any notice of me, young lady,"

François replied at length; " I am too glad to be here to want to eat or drink much."

" Now, come along," said he to Catherine when the table had been cleared; " show me the mill and the house, it seems to me to be rather neglected, and I want to talk to you about it."

And when he had led her outside he questioned her on the state of affairs in an eager fashion and as if he were determined to know everything.

" Ah! François," said Catherine, bursting into tears, " things are as bad as they can be, and if no one comes to the help of my poor mistress, I believe that wicked woman will turn her out and make her spend everything she has in a lawsuit."

" Don't cry, it worries me to hear you," said François; " just try to explain things. What wicked woman do you mean? Madame Sévère?"

" Why, yes! By heaven! She is not content with having ruined our dead master. She lays claim to all he left. She has about fifty ways of getting what she wants. She says Cadet Blanchet owed her money and that when she has sold all we have left she will not have been paid. She sends the bailiffs every day and already expenses are very heavy. Our mistress, to pacify her, has paid all she can and the worry of that after the fatigue of nursing her husband will kill her, I am afraid. Soon we will be without food or fire the way we are going on. The mill-boy has left us because we owed him two years' pay. The mill isn't working, and if that continues we shall lose our customers. They have taken the horses and the harvest; they will be sold, too; all the trees are going to be cut down. Ah! François, it is dreadful."

And she began to cry afresh.

"And what about you, Catherine?" François asked her. "Are you owed money, too? Have your wages been paid?"

"Owed! I!" bellowed Catherine, changing her doleful tone to the roar of a bull. "Never, never! Whether my wages are paid or not is nobody's business."

"Well done, Catherine, well said!" François said to her. "Go on looking after your mistress, and don't worry about anything else. I earned a bit of money in my last place, and I have enough with me to save the horses, the harvest, and the trees. As for the mill, I'll go and have a look at it, and if there is anything wrong I'll soon set it right. Jeannie, who is as swift as a hare, must be on the run from this moment until the evening and to-morrow from daybreak to tell all the customers that the mill is working like ten thousand devils and that the miller is waiting for the flour."

"And what about a doctor for our mistress?"

"I've been thinking about that; but I would rather watch her until to-night to make a decision. You see, Catherine, this is my opinion—doctors are all right when the sick person cannot do without them; but if it is not much of an illness one gets well sooner with God's help than with their drugs. Besides, the doctor's face cures the rich, but it often kills the poor. He pleases and amuses those in easy circumstances, but scares those who only see that face when they are in danger, and that makes them worse. I fancy Madame Blanchet will soon get well when she sees her business set going again.

" And one more thing before we end this conversation, Catherine ; I want to know the truth and you must not mind telling me. It will never come out, and if you remember what I am like you ought to know that a secret is safe with the waif, and I have not changed at all."

" Yes, yes, I know it," said Catherine ; " but why do you consider yourself a waif ? No one calls you that nowadays, François, for you do not deserve to be called it."

" Never mind that. I shall always be what I am, and I am not in the habit of bothering my mind about such things. Tell me what you think of your young mistress, Mariette Blanchet."

" Oh, well. She is a pretty girl. Are you already thinking of marrying her ? She has some property ; her brother could not get at her money for she is a minor, and unless you have come into a fortune, Mr. François . . ."

" Waifs do not come into fortunes," said François, " and as for who is to marry whom, I have no time for thinking about marriage. What I want to get out of you is if the girl is any better than her dead brother, and if Madeleine is pleased with her, or if it is a worry to have her in the house."

" That," said Catherine, " God may be able to tell you, but I can't. Up to the present, she is kindly and thoughtless enough. She likes clothes, lace caps, and dancing. She is not particularly selfish and Madeleine spoils her and treats her so well that she has had no chance to show her teeth. She has never known suffering and we cannot say what will happen to her."

" Was she very fond of her brother ? "

" Not very, except perhaps when he took her to parties; and when our mistress tried to tell him that it was not right to take a decent girl into the company of Madame Sévère, the child, thinking only of her pleasure, caressed her brother and made faces at Madeleine who had to give in. And for that reason Mariette is not as great an enemy of Madame Sévère as I could wish. But you couldn't call her anything but amiable and pleasant to her sister-in-law."

" That will do, Catherine, I don't want to ask you anything else. I forbid you though to say anything of our conversation together to that young girl."

François fulfilled his promises to Catherine. Before the evening Jeannie's diligence had provided corn for milling, and the mill was in working order ; the ice round the mill-wheel was smashed and melted, the machine greased, the broken bits of wood replaced by new ones. François worked until two in the morning and at four he was up again. He tip-toed into Madeleine's room, and found Catherine watching there. He asked her about the sick woman. She had slept well, consoled by the coming of her dear servant and by the help he had brought. And as Catherine refused to leave her mistress before Mariette came to her, François asked at what time the beauty of Cormouer got up.

" Not before daybreak," said Catherine.

" Then you have still two hours to wait, and you will get no sleep at all."

" In the daytime I sleep a little in my chair, or in the barn on the straw while the cows are feeding."

" Well, you are to go to bed now," said François,

"and I will wait here for the young lady, to show her that there are some who go to bed later than she does and who rise earlier. I will busy myself with looking into the papers of the dead man and those which the bailiffs have brought since his death. Where are they?"

"There, in Madeleine's chest," said Catherine. "I will light the lamp for you, François. Come, be brave and try to get us out of this mess since you know all about such writing."

And she went off to bed as obedient to the waif as if he were the master of the house—for it is true that he who is intelligent and good-natured can command people anywhere, and it is his right to do so.

BEFORE setting to work, François, as soon as he was alone with Madeleine and Jeannie, who always slept in the same room as his mother, went to see how the sick woman was sleeping, and he saw she was looking much better than on his arrival. He felt very glad to think that she would not need a doctor and that he alone, by the comfort he brought her, would be able to save her health and amend her lot.

He began to examine the papers and soon realised the intentions of Madame Sévère and saw what was left of Madeleine's property to satisfy her. Besides what Madame Sévère had used up and made Cadet Blanchet squander on her, she claimed a debt of two hundred crowns, and Madeleine had hardly more than that of her own property united with that left to Jeannie by Blanchet—a heritage which had been reduced to the mill and its outbuildings, including the yard, the meadow, the sheds, the garden, the hemp-field and the plantation ; for the fields and all the other land had melted like snow in the hands of Cadet Blanchet.

" Thank God ! " thought François, " I have four hundred crowns with the curé of Aigurande, and if I cannot do better, Madeleine will at least be able to keep her home, the produce of the mill, and what remains of her dowry. But I think I can do better than that. First of all, let me find out if these bills signed by Blanchet for Madame Sévère were not extorted by ruse and begging ; then I can do a business stroke over the lands that have been sold. I know quite well how to manage these things, and according to the names of the present owners, I bet anything I know where I must go to find out where the money is."

The truth is that Blanchet two or three years before his end, embarrassed by his debts to Madame Sévère and pressed for money, had sold his property at a very low price to whoever came along. He had transferred his credit to Madame Sévère thinking thereby to rid himself of her and the friends who had helped her to ruin him. But, as so often happens in such a sale, nearly all those who were in a hurry to buy, attracted by the fertility of the ground, had not a farthing to pay with, and it was with great difficulty that they paid off their interest. Things could have gone on like that for ten or twenty years ; it was money invested, but ill-invested, for Madame Sévère and her friends, and she grumbled a great deal at Cadet Blanchet's hastiness, for she was afraid of not being paid. At all events that is what she said ; but it was a speculation, like any other. A peasant, however miserably poor, will always pay interest, for he is unwilling to let go of what bit of ground he has and which the creditor may take back if he is dissatisfied.

We know all about it, my good folk ! More than once we have had a chance of enriching ourselves by buying good land at a low price. But, low as it may be, it is too high for us. Our covetous eyes are bigger than our purses and we worry ourselves trying to till a field of which the harvest covers barely half the inter-

est exacted by the seller. And when we have slaved
and sweated half our miserable lives we find ourselves
ruined, and only the earth has benefited by our toil
and trouble. The land is worth double, and it is the
moment to sell it. If it sold well we would be saved ;
but that never happens. The interest we have been
paying has sucked us dry so that we have to sell at
once at any price. If we kick against this the courts
force us to do it and the first owner, if he is still alive,
or his representative or inheritors, take back their
property just as it is ; that is to say that for long years
their land has been in our hands and we have been
paying them eight and ten per cent. interest; then they
get it back, worth double because of our labour—a
good piece of land which costs them neither trouble
nor money and the value of which has been increased
by the passage of time. Thus might will always overcome right, and we poor creatures will always be
punished for our covetousness and will remain as
stupid as ever.

In this way Madame Sévère held a mortgage on
her own property and at a good rate of interest.
But she also had Cadet Blanchet's estate under her
thumb, for she had planned so well that the inheritors
of his land succeeded to the mortgage and the payment
devolved on them.

François, seeing through the trick, considered all
means of getting back the land cheaply without ruining
anyone, and doing Madame Sévère and her friends a
bad turn by upsetting their speculation.

It was no easy task. He had enough money to
buy back practically all the land at the price for which
it had been sold. Neither Madame Sévère nor

anybody else could refuse the refund ; it was in the interests of the buyers to resell as quickly as possible and forestall their future ruin. For, let me tell you, listeners, young and old, land bought on credit means certain beggary in your old age. But it is not much good telling you this—it will not lessen your mania for acquisition. No one sees a tilled field in the sun without being in a fever to own it. And that is what François dreaded so much—that burning fever of the peasant who will not be torn from his glebe-land. Do you know what glebe is, my children ? Once upon a time it was much talked of in our parishes. The story went that in the old days the lords bound us to it to sweat us to death, but that the Revolution cut the rope and that we no longer strain like oxen at the master's plough. The truth is that we have merely tied ourselves to our own harrow instead, that we sweat no less, and that we die of it just the same.

The well-to-do townsfolk hereabouts claim that the remedy is never to need or to covet anything. Last Sunday I gave a very good answer to someone who was preaching to me about that—I said if we could be sensible enough, we poor peasants, not to eat, to work the whole time, never to sleep, and to drink the lovely clear water—if the frogs don't mind, that is—we should get on very well, and we would be complimented on our wisdom and good behaviour.

Following the same train of thought, François the waif racked his brains to find a means of making the buyers resell. He decided at last to whisper a lie in their ears—to say that Madame Sévère appeared rich without really being so, that she had more debts than there are holes in a sieve, and that any day her creditors might take over her credit as well as all her property. He meant to tell them this in confidence, and when he had thoroughly scared them he would make Madeleine use his own money to get back the lands at the price which had been paid for them.

At the same time the lie weighed on his conscience until it occurred to him to give a small sum to each of the poor people who had bought the land to compensate them for the interest they had paid. In this way Madeleine would get back her own rights and yet the buyers would be saved from ruin and loss.

He did not trouble about the discredit his story might bring upon Madame Sévère. He argued that a hen is quite right to pull out the feathers of a bird which has destroyed her chickens.

At that moment Jeannie awoke and got up quietly so as not to disturb his mother ; then, after saying good-morning to François, he hurried off to announce to the rest of the customers that the mill was repaired and that there was a new miller working there.

IT was already fully day when Mariette Blanchet rose from her bed, and dressed charmingly in her mourning—such neat black and such clean white that she might have been a little magpie. The poor child was in great trouble because her mourning prevented her, for a time, from going to dances and all the young men would be miserable without her ; she was so good-hearted that she felt extremely sorry for them.

"What ! " she said, seeing François tidying papers in Madeleine's room, " you are taking over the whole thing here, Mr. Miller ; you make flour, transact business, cook the gruel ; we shall soon see you sewing and spinning . . ."

" And you, young lady," said François, observing that she was admiring him with her eyes as she chaffed him with her tongue, " I haven't yet noticed you spinning or sewing ; I fancy you will soon sleep until midday ; that will be very good for you. It keeps the complexion fresh."

" Hullo, Mr. François, so we are already uttering home truths. . . . Beware of that game ; I can play it too."

" At your service, young lady."

" All in good time ; don't be afraid, my fine miller. But what has become of Catherine that you are acting sick-nurse ? Wouldn't you like a skirt and a cap ? "

" No doubt you would want a miller's blouse and hat, then, to go to the mill ? For, as you don't do the woman's job, which is to watch for a while by your sister's bed, you wish to turn the straw and work the mill. At your service. Let us exchange clothing."

" You appear to be trying to teach me a lesson ? "

" No, you taught me one first, and that is why, out of honesty, I return that which you lent me."

" Good ! good ! You like to laugh and joke. But you choose the wrong moment. We are not merry here. Not long since we were at the cemetery. And if you chatter so much you will disturb my sister-in-law who is in sore need of respose."

" For that very reason you should not raise your voice, young lady ; I am speaking very softly to you, and you are not just now talking in the proper tones for a sick-room."

" That will do, if you please," said Mariette, dropping her voice, but growing red all the same ; " do me the kindness of seeing if Catherine is anywhere about, and tell me why she left my sister-in-law in your care."

" I beg your pardon, young lady," said François, without getting heated at all. " But since you are so fond of sleep it was impossible to leave her in your care, so she had to be confided to me. And as for summoning the poor woman—I won't, for she is overcome with fatigue. Without offence, I must remind you that she has been up for a fortnight. I sent her to bed, and I intend to do her work as well as my own until midday, for it is only fair that we should help one another."

" Listen, Mr. François," said the girl with a sudden

change of tone, " you appear to want to tell me that I think only of myself and that I leave all the bother to others. Perhaps truly I ought to have sat up in my turn had Catherine said she was tired. But she said she wasn't at all, and I did not think my sister-in-law so dangerously ill. It seems you judge me to be unkind, but I don't know why. You have only known me since yesterday, and we have not been on sufficiently familiar terms to justify you taking me up in that way. You behave too much as if you were the head of the family—whereas really . . ."

" Go on, say it, my lovely Mariette ; say what is on the tip of your tongue. And really I was brought up by charity—isn't that it ? and I can't be a member of the family, for I have no family ; I haven't the right, being a waif ! Is that all you would like to say ? "

As he gave Mariette this direct challenge François scrutinised her face in a way that made her blush to the roots of her hair, for she saw that he was speaking as a man who is angered and in earnest, although at the same time he appeared so quiet and mild that she felt he could not answer back or speak or think unjustly.

The poor girl felt a little afraid—she who was so sharp with her tongue as a rule—but her fear did not detract from her desire to appear pleasing in the eyes of this handsome youth who spoke so sternly and looked at her with such frankness. She felt so dumbfounded and embarrassed that she had hard work to restrain her tears and hastily turned away lest François should see her emotion.

But he had noticed it already, and said to her in a friendly voice : " You have not annoyed me a bit,

Mariette, and you have no need to be annoyed either. I don't think ill of you. I only feel that you are young, that the house is in a bad way, and that it doesn't seem to trouble you, and I must tell you what I think."

"Well, what do you think ? " she exclaimed : " let us have it all at one blow so that we know if you are a friend or an enemy."

" I think that if you don't care to take a little trouble and pains about one you love and who is in a bad state, you had better get out of the way, leave everything, think about your fine clothes, your lovers, your future marriage ; but don't be surprised if other people get on with your job here. But if you are kind-hearted, my dear child, if you love your sister-in-law and your good little nephew, and even the poor servant who is ready to die in harness like a faithful horse, you must get up a bit earlier in the morning, look after Madeleine, comfort Jeannie, relieve Catherine, and, above all, do not listen to Madame Sévère who is the enemy of this house—a bad woman, believe me. That is what I think, no more than that."

" I am very glad to hear it," said Mariette, a little drily, " and now perhaps you will tell me what right you have to urge me to think as you do."

" Oh ! is that the way you take it ? " François replied. " My right is the waif's right, and—you ought to know this—the right of the child brought up here by the charitableness of Madame Blanchet : that fact gives me the right to love her as my mother, and the right to act in such a way that she is rewarded for her kindness."

" I don't blame you for that," replied Mariette,

" and I see that I can't do better than to offer you my esteem at the moment and my friendship later on."

" I am glad of that," said François. " Won't you shake hands on it ? "

And he went towards her with outstretched hand and no sign of embarrassment. But the silly child felt suddenly coquettish, and, taking her hand away, remarked that it was not nice for a young girl to give her hand to a boy.

François laughed at that and let her go, knowing that she could not behave simply, and that she thought first and foremost of seeking his admiration.

" Well, my girl," he thought, " you won't have any luck there, and neither will we be friends according to your lights."

He went towards Madeleine who had just woken up, and who said to him, taking both his hands in hers :

" I have slept well, my son, and I am glad your face is the first I see on waking ; but why is my Jeannie not with you ? "

Then when matters had been explained to her she spoke kindly to Mariette, fearing that the girl might have sat up all night with her, and assured her there was no need to take so much care of her in such a slight illness. Mariette expected François to say that she had really got up very late, but he said nothing, and left her alone with Madeleine who was anxious to try to dress as she no longer felt feverish.

She felt so well at the end of three days that she could talk business with François.

" Don't worry, my dear mother," he said to her ; " I grew out of my stupidity a little over there, and

I know how things should be done. I want to get
your affairs straight again, and I am going to see
things through. Let me do it, don't give the lie to
anything I may say, and sign all the things I give you
to sign. Now that I am less troubled about your
health I am going to the town to see the lawyers. It
is market day, and I shall meet the folk I want to see,
and I reckon I shall not waste my time."

He did as he had promised; and when he had
received advice from the lawyers he saw that the last
bills signed by Blanchet for Madame Sévère could be
very useful in a lawsuit, since he had signed them in
an unfit state, being fuddled with fever, wine, and
stupidity. Madame Sévère imagined that Madeleine
would not take it to court because of the cost. François had no intention of urging Madeleine to do so,
but he thought a suitable arrangement could be made
by going about things in a friendly way at first; and
since he had to have someone to visit the enemy he
thought of a plan which succeeded admirably.

He had noticed for the last three days that young
Mariette was in the habit of going for a daily walk
round by Dollins, where Madame Sévère lived, and
that she was on better terms than he would have
wished with that woman, simply because she met
there young people of her acquaintance and well-to-
do folk who murmured flattery in her ear. It was
not that she really wanted to listen to them; she
was still an innocent girl and thought no evil could
befall her. But she liked compliments as a cat likes
cream. She hid her walks from Madeleine; and as
the latter never gossiped with other women, and
was not yet out of her room, she did not notice any-

thing amiss and never suspected the girl. Catherine was not the woman to guess or notice the least thing. The little wretch laid her plans so well that on the pretext of taking the flock to graze, she went off to enjoy herself in bad company, and left the sheep in the care of some little shepherd-boy.

François going about his work at the mill noticed this, said nothing about it at the house, and made use of it in the following manner.

HE went and planted himself in her path, at the ford, and as she crossed the bridge on the way to Dollins, she found the waif astride the middle of it with one leg overhanging the river at each side and on his face the expression of a man who has plenty of time at his disposal. She became as red as a poppy, and if she had had time to pretend to be there by chance she would have turned aside. But the bridge was hidden by branches, and so she did not see the enemy until she was in his clutches. He was facing her, and she saw no hope of going on or retreating without being seen.

" Hullo ! Mister Miller," she cried, to see what boldness would do. " Won't you move aside a bit to let other folks go by ? "

" No, young lady," replied François, " for I am the guardian of the bridge for this evening, and I collect toll of all who wish to pass."

" Are you crazy, François ? You don't pay toll in this part of the country, and no one has the right of way over any bridge or whatever you call them in your Aigurande. But you may say what you please so long as you remove yourself as quickly as you can ; this isn't the place for fooling ; you will make me fall into the water."

" Then," François, without moving away, and folding his arms on his chest, " you think that I

147

want to fool with you and that my toll fee will be to say sweet nothings to you ? Get rid of that idea, young lady : I want to talk sensibly to you, and I will allow you to pass over if you will let me accompany you to the end of the road to talk to you."

"That will not suit me at all," said Mariette, a little fluttered at the thought of what François might be going to say to her. "What would they say of me if I were seen alone on the road with a boy to whom I am not even engaged ? "

"You are right," said François. "Since Madame Sévère is not here to guarantee your reputation you might be talked about ; that is why you are going to see her, so that you may walk about her garden with all your admirers. Oh, well, so as not to embarrass you I will tell you here, in two words, what I have to say, for it is important—and this is it : You are a good girl, you are fond of your sister-in-law, Madeleine ; you see that she is in trouble, and you would like to help her, is that not so ? "

" If that is what you want to talk to me about I will listen to you, for it is quite true," replied Mariette.

"Well, my dear young lady," said François, rising and leaning with her against the side of the little bridge, " you can do Madame Blanchet a great service. I like to think that it is towards her happiness and in her interest that you are friendly with Madame Sévère, and, that being so, you must get her to agree to a certain arrangement. She requires two things which she can't in reason have at one and the same time : first to make Miller Blanchet's estates the surety for the payment of the lands he sold to pay her : second, to exact payment for the promissory-notes in her favour. It is of no use for her to squeeze and press that miserable little heritage, she will never get out of it what she wants. Make it clear to her that if she does not insist that we guarantee the payment of the land we can pay the notes, but that if she does not free us from the one debt we will not be able to pay her the other ; and that in making charges which will exhaust our means without profit to her, she risks losing the lot."

" That seems to me quite obvious," said Mariette ; " although I do not know anything about business matters, I can understand that much. And if I happen to persuade her, François, which would be better for my sister-in-law, to pay the notes or to be obliged to redeem the security ? "

" It would be worse to have to pay the notes for that would be more unjust. We could protest against paying the notes and go to law about it ; but a lawsuit costs money, and you know there is none in the house and that there never will be any. Thus, whether your sister-in-law's money goes in a lawsuit, or in payment to Madame Sévère, it is all one to her, whereas it is to Madame Sévère's advantage to be paid without a lawsuit. As she will be ruined in any case Madeleine would rather have all she has taken from her than have round her neck the mill-stone of a debt which might last a life-time ; for the buyers of Cadet Blanchet's land are not likely to pay up. This is known to Madame Sévère, and one day she will have to take back those lands ; not that that upsets her, for it is profitable to her to find them improved and to have had the interest on them at the same time. So you see Madame Sévère is not losing anything by giving us our freedom, and she thus assures the payment of her bills."

"I will do as you tell me," said Mariette, "and if I fail you need have no respect for me."

"Well then, good luck, Mariette, and a pleasant walk," said François, stepping out of her way.

Mariette went to Dollins, very glad of a good excuse for appearing and for staying a while and for returning there during the next few days. Madame Sévère pretended to take in what she said, but in her heart she decided to be in no hurry about it. She had always hated Madeleine Blanchet for the respect which her husband had been obliged to give her in spite of himself. She thought she had her in the hollow of her hand for the rest of her life, and she would rather have given up the payment of the bills that she knew very well were not worth much than forgo the pleasure of tormenting her with the burden of an endless debt.

François knew this quite well, and he wanted to bring her to the point of claiming payment for this debt so that he could repurchase Jeannie's excellent property from those who had bought it for practically nothing. But when Mariette returned with her message, he realised that they were trying to put him off with words ; that, on the one hand the child would be pleased to prolong the commission, and that, on the other hand, Madame Sévère had not yet reached the point of preferring the ruin of Madeleine to the payment of her bills.

To bring things to a climax, he took Mariette aside a couple of days later: "It is no good going to Dollins to-day, my dear young lady," said he. "Your sister-in-law has heard, I don't know how, that you are often there, and she says it is not the right place for a well-brought-up girl. I tried to get her to see that you are going there in her own interests, but she blamed me as much as you. She said that she would rather be ruined than see you dishonoured, that you are in her charge, and that she has authority over you. You will be forcibly prevented if you do not give up going of your own accord. She will say nothing about it if you do not go back, for she does not wish to be unkind to you, but she is very angry with you and you really ought to ask her pardon."

François had set her off. He was right in his estimation of Mariette's temper, which was as hasty and inflammable as her brother's had been.

" Oh ! ought I, indeed ! " she exclaimed. " Fancy obeying one's sister-in-law like a three-year-old child. Anyone would think she was my mother, and I ought to obey her ! And what makes her think I may lose my honour ? Kindly tell her that it is as firmly established as hers, and better perhaps. What does she know of Madame Sévère, who is as good as anybody else ? One need not be dishonest if one does not sit all day sewing, spinning, and saying one's prayers. My sister-in-law is unjust to her because they are at variance over money-matters, and she thinks she can treat me as she pleases. It is unwise of her, for if Madame Sévère were so minded she would turn her out of house and home ; and it proves that Madame Sévère is less bad than her reputation, that she does not do this, but is patient. And I, who was good enough to act as go-between—look what thanks I get ! Come, come, François, remember that the most respectable folk are not always the most prudish, and that I do no worse in going to Madame Sévère than in stopping here."

"That remains to be seen!" said François, who wanted to bring things to a head; "your sister-in-law is very likely right in thinking that you are up to no good. And, look here, Mariette, I see you that are too keen on going there again, and that won't do at all. What you had to say about Madeleine's affairs has been said, and if Madame Sévère does not respond that means she does not want to respond. Then do not go there again, or I will believe, with Madeleine, that you are going there with no good intentions."

"Then you have decided, Mr. François," said Mariette in a fury, "that you are going to dictate to me as well. You think you are the master of the house in the place of my brother. You are not yet bearded enough to be in a position to rebuke me, and I warn you to leave me alone. Good-bye to you," she added, readjusting her cap; "if my sister-in-law wants me you can tell her that I am with Madame Sévère, and if she sends you to look for me, you will see what your reception will be."

Thereupon she slammed the door, and tripped lightly over to Dollins; but François was afraid her anger would have time to cool on the way, especially as the weather was frosty, and he let her get ahead; then, as she drew near Madame Sévère's house, he shot off like an arrow from a bow and caught her up, making her think Madeleine had sent him after her.

There he gibed her until she raised her hand to strike him, but he dodged the blows, knowing that her anger would fall with every stroke, for a woman who beats anyone is cured of her ill-temper. He ran off then, and as soon as she was with Madame Sévère she made a great fuss. The poor child had no ill intentions, but in the first ardour of her fury she did not know how to keep calm, and she put Madame Sévère in such a rage that François, who was going slowly along the hollow road, heard them from the other side of the hemp-field, sizzling and crackling like a fire in a hayloft.

THINGS turned out as he wished, and he was so satisfied that he went to Aigurande the next day, got his money from the curé, and returned the same night with his four crisp scraps of paper worth so much and making as little sound in his pocket as a crumb of bread. A week later they heard from Madame Sévère. All the purchasers of Blanchet's land were called upon to pay ; none of them could, and Madeleine was threatened with having to do so in their stead.

As soon as she realised this she came in full of fear, for François had said nothing of his plans.

" Good ! " he said, rubbing his hands, " the merchant does not always gain, nor the thief always get away with the spoil. Madame Sévère is going to have bad luck and you are going to come off well. Never mind, my dear mother, go on as if you thought you were ruined. The more you suffer the better pleased she will be to do what she thinks will turn out ill for you. But this loss is your gain, for you are going, by paying Madame Sévère, to get back all your son's property."

" And how do you suppose I am to pay for this, my child ? "

" With the money which is in my pocket, and which is yours."

Madeleine wanted to forbid him ; but the waif was

stubborn, he said, and no one could turn him from his purpose. He dashed off to the lawyer to make over his two hundred crowns to Widow Blanchet, and Madame Sévère was paid, however she liked it, as were the other creditors who were in league with her.

And even when François had carried out his intention of indemnifying the poor buyers he had still enough money left to go to court, and he told Madame Sévère that he was going to start a lawsuit about the promissory notes she had got the dead man to sign by means of fraud. He spread a story which created a sensation in those parts. He said that in examining an old wall of the mill with a view to propping it up he had come across a money-box belonging to the dead Madame Blanchet and full of ancient gold coins, which made Madeleine richer than she had ever been. So Madame Sévère, overcome, agreed to an arrangement, hoping that François had control of some of this money found so opportunely, and that by being on good terms with him she might be able to lay hands on more than he exhibited to her. But she had her trouble for nothing, and he dealt so harshly with her that she was obliged to give up the bills for a hundred crowns.

By way of revenge she stirred Mariette by telling her that the money-box which belonged to old Mother Blanchet ought to be divided between her and Jeannie, that she had a right to it, and that she ought to go to court against her sister-in-law.

Thus the waif was forced to tell the truth about the source of the money he had furnished, and the curé of Aigurande sent him the proofs in case of a lawsuit.

First he showed these proofs to Mariette, beseeching

her not to spread the story uselessly, and telling her that the best thing she could do would be to keep quiet. But Mariette did not keep quiet at all. Her brain was on fire with all these upsets in the family, and the poor child was terribly tempted. In spite of Madeleine's goodness to her and the fact that she treated her as if she were her own daughter, forgiving her all her moods, she disliked her sister-in-law and was jealous of her for a reason which she was ashamed to own. The truth is that in the course of her arguments and furies with François she had slowly become fond of him, without realising the change in her feelings. The more he lectured her for her caprices and her shortcomings the more eager she became to please him.

She was not the sort of girl to become embittered by her grief or even to melt into tears; but she was for ever thinking that François, a handsome lad, rich, honest, kind to everyone, and very capable, was brave enough to give the last drop of his blood for the woman he loved; and that woman was not herself, although she could say that she was the prettiest and richest girl in the neighbourhood, and that she had dozens of suitors.

One day she opened her heart to her false friend Madame Sévère. It was in the pasture at the end of the road of Napes.* There is an old apple-tree there and it was in flower, for while this had been going on they had reached the month of May, and as Mariette was watching her flock at the river-side Madame Sévère came to chat with her under the apple-blossom.

* Nénufar, Nymphéa, Napée=Nenuphar, water-lily.

But, by the mercy of Providence, François happened to be passing and overheard their words ; for, seeing Madame Sévère go into the field he guessed she had gone there to concoct some mischief against Madeleine; and as the river was low he walked noiselessly along the bank behind some of the bushes which grow so high in those parts that a hay-cart would be hidden behind them. Once there he sat down on the sand holding his breath and listening with all his ears.

And this is what those two female tongues gossiped about. First Mariette said that of all her suitors none pleased her because of a miller, by no means gallant, but the only one who kept her awake at night. Madame Sévère, however, wanted to marry her to a young man she knew who was so anxious to have the girl that he had promised her a fine present if she could manage to bring off a marriage between him and little Mariette Blanchet. Apparently she had even exacted a first instalment from him of this gift (as similarly from many others), so she did her best to sicken Mariette of François.

"A plague on the waif !" she said to her, "What, Mariette, a girl in your position marry a foundling ! You would be called Madame Strawberry, for he has no other name. I should be ashamed for you, you poor creature. And, besides, you haven't a chance, for you would have to dispute him with your sister-in-law and he is her lover—as true as I stand here."

"Why, Madame Sévère," cried Mariette, "you have more than once given me to understand that, but I can't believe it ; my sister-in-law is too old."

"No, no, Mariette ; your sister-in-law is not too old for that ; she is hardly thirty, and this waif was only an urchin when your brother found him very friendly with his wife. That is why one day he thrashed him soundly with the butt of his whip and sent him away."

François was dying to jump over the bushes and tell Madame Sévère that she lied, but he desisted and stayed quiet.

And then Madame Sévère said all sorts of things about him, credited him with lies and evil ways, so that François grew scarlet and could scarcely contain himself.

"Then," said Mariette, "he intends to marry her now that she is a widow. He has already given her a good deal of his money and he would like at least to be able to enjoy that which he has bought back."

"But he will not be the highest bidder," said the other, "for Madeleine will look for someone richer now that she has got all she can out of him, and she will find someone. She must get a man to look after her property, and, while she is looking round for one, she keeps this great fool with her who serves her for nothing, and who relieves the tedium of her widowhood."

"If that is the way she behaves," said Mariette resentfully, "what a disreputable house I am living in! It will be no loss to leave it. Do you know, Madame Sévère, I am in very queer sort of house, and people will speak ill of me. Indeed, I can't stay there; I must get away. Ah, well, these religious folk talk ill of others and are secretly shameless themselves. I advise her not to speak badly of you and me after this.

"Well, I will say good-bye to her, and I will come to live with you. If she doesn't like it I will deal with her, and if she wants to force me to go back to her she must go to law about it, and I'll show her up then, do you understand ? "

" There is a better remedy, Mariette, and that is to get married as soon as you can. She will not refuse her consent for she is in a hurry, I am sure, to get rid of you. You interfere with her affair with the fine waif. And you must not hesitate, do you see, or it will be said that he belongs to you both and no one will want to marry you then. Get married to the man I advise you to take."

" So I will ! " cried Mariette, breaking her shepherdess-crook against the old apple-tree. " I give you my word. Go and find him, Madame Sévère, and send him to the house this evening to ask my hand, and let our banns be published next Sunday."

AS François climbed up the river bank where he had
been in hiding listening to this feminine gossip,
he was unhappier than ever before. His heart felt
as heavy as lead, and half-way home he lost the
courage to enter the house, and went along the road of
Napes to sit down in the little spinney of oaks at the
end of the meadow.

Once alone there he wept like a child, broken-
hearted with grief and shame, for he was deeply
ashamed of the accusation against himself and poor
Madeleine whom he had loved with such chaste
devotion all his life, getting nothing out of it in the
end but the cruelty of evil tongues.

" My God, my God ! " he said to himself, " how
can the world be so wicked, and a woman like Madame
Sévère have the impertinence to measure the honour
of a woman like my dear mother by her own standards ?
And even that young fool, Mariette, who should be
innocent and decent-minded, for she is but a child, and
does not understand the meaning of evil, listens to
these devilries and believes them as if she knew all
about such things ! Others think it too, in that case,
and, as most of those who live this mortal life think evil
exists everywhere, I suppose nearly everybody will
think that because I love Madame Blanchet and she
loves me it is a question of our being lovers together."

Thereupon poor François began to examine his

conscience and search his memory very deeply to see
if his behaviour towards Madeleine had done anything
to foster the evil ideas in Madame Sévère's mind.
Whether he had always acted wisely and, for lack of
discretion and prudence, given anyone reason to think
ill. But search as he might he could not find an
instance of anything of the kind, for he had never
thought in those terms.

And then, absorbed and dreamy, he murmured to
himself: "Well, and suppose my friendship had
turned to love, what harm would there be in that now
she is a widow and free to marry again? I have given
her and Jeannie a good part of my money, but I still
have enough to be a good match and she would not
wrong her child in taking me for her husband. It
would not be so very ambitious of me to aspire to that,
no one could say I love her for her money. Certainly
I am a waif, but she does not mind about that. She
has loved me as if I were her son and that is the deepest
of all affections; she could quite well love me in another
way. I can see that her enemies will oblige me to
leave her if I do not marry her; and I would die
sooner than leave her again. Besides, she still needs
me and it would be cowardly to leave so much on her
hands when there are mine, as well as my money, at her
service. Yes, all that is mine should be hers, and
since she often talks of recompensing me in the end, I
must put that idea out of her head by giving her an
equal share with me in the eyes of God and the law.
Yes, of course, she must keep her good name for the
sake of her son and only by marrying will she not lose
it. Why did I not think of it before, why did that
wicked tongue have to put it into my mind? I was

too big a fool, too unsuspecting, and my poor mother is so good to others that she does not mind suffering at all herself. But all is for the best under the will of heaven, and Madame Sévère seeking to do me a bad turn has done me the kindness to point out my duty to me."

And, without wondering or considering further, François went back determined to speak to Madame Blanchet at once about his project, and to ask her on his knees to take him as her protector in the name of God and for eternity.

But when he got to Cormouer he saw Madeleine spinning her wool on the threshold of her door and for the first time in his life her face struck him with fear and uncertainty. Instead of going to her at once as usual and looking into her eyes with a frank gaze and asking her how she felt, he stopped on the little bridge as if he were examining the weir and watched her out of the corner of his eye. When she turned to him he looked the other way, not knowing himself what was the matter with him and why a thing which had seemed so simple and homely a little while ago should have become so hard to confess.

Then Madeleine called him, saying :

" Come over here, François. We are all alone, so come and sit by my side and open your heart to me as to a father confessor, for I want the truth out of you."

This speech of Madeleine's quite comforted François, and sitting down beside her, he said :

" Be assured, my dear mother, that I will open my heart to you as to God, and that you will hear nothing but the truth in my confession."

And he imagined that perhaps she had heard something which had brought her to the same conclusion as himself. This made him feel quite happy and he waited for her to speak.

"François," said she, "you are twenty-one now, and you ought to think of settling down ; have you any objection to that ? "

"No, no, I have no other idea than yours," replied François, blushing with pleasure, "go on, my dear Madeleine."

"Very well," she went on, "I was waiting for you to tell me something, and I really believe that I know what would suit you. Well, since it is your wish it is also mine, and may be I thought of it before you did. I waited to see if the person in question would fall in love with you, and I fancy that if she does not care for you yet she soon will. Don't you think so too, and won't you tell me how far things have gone ? . . . Why are you looking at me with that startled expression ? Haven't I made myself sufficiently clear ? But I see you are shy, and I must help you out. Well, the poor child has been sulking all morning because you teased her a bit last evening, and perhaps she imagines you do not love her. But I have seen that you love her, and if you reproach her a little for her silly ways it is because you feel rather jealous. Do not let that stop you, François. She is young and pretty, which is dangerous, but if she really loved you she would soon learn to obey you."

"I would very much like to know," said François, unhappily, "of whom you are speaking, my dear mother, for I don't understand a word."

"Really ? " said Madeleine, "you don't know ? Did I dream it, or are you wanting to keep it secret from me ? "

"A secret from you?" said François, taking Madeleine's hand; then he let it go and took a corner of her apron which he crushed as if he were irritated; he held it to his lips as if he wanted to kiss it, and then let it go as he had loosed her hand, for he felt like weeping, falling into a rage, and then rather faint; all these emotions passed in quick succession.

"Why," said Madeleine, astonished, "you are unhappy, my child, which proves that you are in love and that things are not going as you would like. But I assure you that Mariette is good-hearted, that she is unhappy too, and that if you were to tell her frankly what you feel, she on her side would tell you that she thinks of no one but you."

François stood up, and without saying a word began to walk up and down the yard, and then he returned and said to Madeleine:

"I am astonished at what is in your mind, Madame Blanchet. As for me, I have never thought of such a thing, and I know very well that Miss Mariette neither cares for nor esteems me."

"Come, come," said Madeleine, "disappointment makes you talk like that, my child. Have I not seen you chatting with her, watched you say words incomprehensible to me, but which she appeared to understand for she blushed like fire? Do I not know that she leaves the meadow every day and gives her flock to anyone's charge? Our crops suffer if her sheep gain; but I would rather not restrain her nor talk to her about sheep when her brain is all on fire with thoughts of love and marriage. The poor child is at an age when one does not look after one's flocks very well, and controls one's heart still less easily. But it is a great piece of luck for her, François, that instead of being infatuated with one of these bad lots I feared she would meet at Madame Sévère's she has had the good sense to fall in love with you. I, too, am very glad to think that, married to my sister-in-law whom I regard almost as a daughter, you would live and work near me, you would be in my family, and I could discharge my debt to you for all the good you have done by having you to live here, in doing things for you, and bringing up your children. Therefore do not destroy the happiness I have built up by childish nonsense. Try to see clearly and cure yourself of your jealousy. If Mariette likes to make herself look pretty it is to charm you. If she is a bit careless lately it is that she is thinking too much about you, and if sometimes she talks to me in too lively a fashion it is because she is in a temper at your teasing and does not know on whom to avenge herself. But that she wants to be sensible and that she is good-natured is proved by the fact that she realises how kind and good you are and that she wants to have you for her husband."

"You are good, my dear mother," said François, saddened; "yes, you are good, for you believe in the goodness of others; but you are mistaken. I can tell you that if Mariette is good too, and I will not deny it, fearing to make mischief between you, it is another kind of goodness, quite unlike yours, and which, for that reason, I do not appreciate at all. Then do not talk to me about her. I swear faithfully to you that I am no more in love with her than I am with old Catherine, and that if she cares for me it is very unfortunate because I do not feel that way at all.

"Do not say anything to her to make her admit that she loves me. It would be unwise and you would make us enemies. On the contrary, you must listen to what she has to say to you this evening and let her marry Jean Aubard—for she has decided to do so. Let her get married as soon as possible ; it is no good her staying with you. She does not like it and it gives you no pleasure."

"Jean Aubard ! " said Madeleine, "he won't suit her ; he is a very stupid fellow, and she is too clever to submit to a man with no brains."

"He is rich and she won't submit to him. She will order him about and he is just the man for her. Won't you believe your friend, my dear mother ? You know I have never given you bad advice. Let this young woman go, for she does not love you as she should, and she does not realise your true worth."

"It is disappointment which makes you talk like this, François," said Madeleine, putting her hand on his head and shaking it a little as if to force the truth out of it. But François, angered that she would not believe him, drew back and said to her in a discontented voice that it was the first time in his life he had had an argument with her :

"You are not fair to me, Madame Blanchet. I tell you that this girl does not like you. You force me to say it against my will for I did not come here to stir up strife between you. But I tell it you because I know it to be true. And you still think I love her ? Why, it must be you who do not love me any longer since you will not believe me."

And, sick with grief, François went to weep alone by the fountain.

MADELEINE was even more upset than François and would have liked to go to him and question him further and comfort him, but she was prevented by the entrance of Mariette who came with an odd expression on her face to speak to her about Jean Aubard, and tell her of his offer of marriage. Madeleine could not overcome the notion that all this savoured of a lovers' quarrel and tried to speak to her of François; thereupon Mariette replied in a tone which made her very unhappy and which she could not understand:

"Let those who love waifs keep them for their own amusement. As for me, I am a decent girl and if my poor brother *is* dead I will not allow my honour to be insulted. I am quite independent, Madeleine, and if the law forces me to ask your advice it does not force me to take it when you advise me ill. I ask you therefore not to refuse me now for I could cross *you* later on."

"I do not know what is the matter with you, my poor child," said Madeleine very sweetly but sadly, "you speak to me as if you neither esteemed nor cared for me. I think that you are in some trouble which has dazed you for the time. I beseech you to take two or three days to think it over. I will tell Jean Aubard to come back, and if you feel the same after you have thought about it in quietness I will make no objection to your marriage as he is a decent man and comfortably off. But you are so upset that you cannot know your own mind nor judge of the affection I have for you. I feel very sad and I see that you do too, so I will forgive you."

Mariette tossed her head as a sign that she scorned such a pardon and she went to put on her silk apron to receive Jean Aubard, who came an hour later with the buxom Madame Sévère in her best clothes.

Madeleine then began to think that Mariette must dislike her if she could bring into her house on a family matter a woman who was her enemy and whom she could not see without blushing. She behaved, however, very pleasantly as she met her and offered her refreshment without showing spite or rancour. She was afraid of driving Mariette to extremes in going against her. She said that she would not oppose the wishes of her sister-in-law, but that she asked three days before giving an answer.

Upon which Madame Sévère remarked insolently that it was a very long time ; and Madeleine responded quietly that it was very short. And then Jean Aubard went off looking as stupid as possible and giggling like a simpleton, for he never doubted that Mariette was madly in love with him. He had paid for that belief and Madame Sévère had given him his money's worth.

As she went, the latter remarked to Mariette that she was having some pancakes made at her house to celebrate the engagement and that even if Madame Blanchet withheld her permission the feast must be eaten. Madeleine pointed out that it was not customary for a young girl to go with a youth to whom permission had not yet been accorded.

" In that case I won't go," said Mariette, feeling very provoked.

" But of course you will, you must come," cried Madame Sévère, " are you not your own mistress ? "

" No, no," retorted Mariette, " don't you see that my sister-in-law has commanded me to stay at home ? "

And she went into the room, slamming the door. But she only walked through it and, going out of the house by the backway, she rejoined Madame Sévère and the young man at the end of the field, laughing and insolent.

Poor Madeleine could not help crying when she saw how things were.

" François is right," she thought ; " that child does not care for me and is ungrateful. She will not understand that I act for the best for her, that I seek her happiness, and that I want to prevent her from doing something that she will regret. She has listened to bad counsel, and I am forced to see that wretched Sévère bring malice and misery into my family. I have done nothing to deserve all this trouble, and I must resign myself to the will of God. Luckily my poor François saw more clearly than I. He would have suffered had he taken such a wife ! "

She went to look for him to tell him what she thought, but she found him weeping near the fountain, and, imagining that he was unhappy about Mariette, she told him that she could console him. The more she talked, however, the more miserable she made him, for he saw that she would not understand the truth and that she could not feel for him as he wanted her to feel.

That evening after Jeannie was in bed and asleep

169

in the room, François stayed a while with Madeleine trying to explain. He said to begin with that Mariette was jealous of her, that Madame Sévère said infamous things and told abominable lies.

But Madeleine did not see anything in this.

" What could they say about me ? " she asked simply ; " what could put jealousy into the head of that poor little fool of a Mariette ? You are mistaken, François, it is something else, some reason we shall learn later on. As for jealousy, that is impossible ; I am too old to stand in the way of a young and pretty girl. I am nearly thirty, and for a peasant woman who has had a great deal of trouble and worry that is old enough to be your mother. Only a devil dare say that I look on you as other than a son, and Mariette must have seen that I wanted her to marry you. No, no, don't believe that she thought such wicked things, or don't tell me about them, my child. It would cause me too much shame and misery."

" However," said François, forcing himself to go on, and bending over the hearth so that Madeleine should not see his confusion, " Miller Blanchet thought such wicked things when he made me leave the house."

" You know that now then, François ? " said Madeleine. " How do you know ? I never told you and I would never have told you. If Catherine has mentioned it she had no business to. Such an idea must shock and pain you as it did me. But do not let us think about it any more and let us forgive my dead husband for it. The shame falls on Madame Sévère, but she can no longer be jealous of me. I have no husband. I am as old and ugly as she could

desire nowadays ; and I do not mind, for that gives
me the right to be respected, to treat you as my son,
and to look for a nice young woman for you who would
be glad to live here and who would love me as her
mother. That is all I ask, François, and it will come
to us—don't worry. So much the worse for Mariette
if she scorns the happiness I would have given her.

"Go to bed now, my child, and take heart again.
If I thought I stood in the way of your marriage I
would send you away at once ; but you can be sure
no one will gossip about me, for one never imagines
the impossible."

Listening to Madeleine, François thought she must
be right, he was so used to believing her. He got up
to say good night and to go, but, taking her hand,
for the first time he thought of looking to see if she
was old and ugly. She was so serious and sad she
deceived herself about her appearance, for she was as
pretty as she had ever been.

Suddenly François saw that she was young and found
her perfectly beautiful, and his heart began to thump
as if he had been climbing into a belfry. He went to
sleep in the mill where he had his bed among the sacks
of flour, hemmed in with a square of planks. When
he was alone there he began to tremble and gasp as
if he had a fever. He was lovesick. For the first
time in his life he was scorched by the great flame
which had gently warmed him up till now.

FROM that moment the waif was so sad that it was pitiful to see him. He worked as much as four men, but he was no longer joyful, nor did he get any rest, and Madeleine could not make him say what was the matter with him. It was of no use for him to swear that he neither loved nor regretted Mariette, Madeleine would not believe him and could find no other reason for his misery. She was sorry to see him suffering and not to be in his confidence as usual, and it astonished her very much that the young man was so obstinate and proud in his trouble.

As hers was not a tormenting nature she determined not to speak of it again to him. She tried to make Mariette come round, but she was so ill-received that she lost courage and desisted, sick at heart, but anxious not to show her pain lest she should add to the unhappiness of others.

François went on serving her and helping her with the same courage and devotion as before. As of old he was with her as much as possible. But he did not talk to her in the old way. He was always confused in her presence. He became as red as fire and as white as snow all in the same minute, so, often, indeed that she thought him ill and took his wrist to see if he were feverish; but he drew back as if her touch hurt him and sometimes he reproached her in words she did not understand.

Every day this trouble grew between them. Preparations for Mariette's marriage with Jean Aubard were going on, and the day on which she would terminate her period of mourning was that fixed for the wedding. Madeleine dreaded that day for she was afraid that François would be driven mad, and she wanted to send him to his old master, Jean Vertaud, at Aigurande, for a time to distract him from his misery. But François was anxious that Mariette should not think in the same terms as Madeleine was determined to think. He showed no sign of grief in her presence. He was friendly with the young man, and when he met Madame Sévère in the road he joked with her to show her that he had no fear of her. He was present at the wedding; and, as he was obviously glad to see that girl leave their house and to have Madeleine rid of a false friend, no one thought he had ever had any love for her.

Madeleine herself began to think this must be the case, or at least to imagine that he must have got over it. She said good-bye to Mariette with her usual good nature, but that young woman, feeling jealous of her on account of the waif, took care to show her that she left her without regret or kindly feelings. Accustomed as she was to being hurt, good Madeleine wept for this naughtiness and prayed God for her.

At the end of a week François suddenly announced that he had business at Aigurande and that he was going away for five or six days, which did not astonish her and even pleased her; she thought a change would do him good for he seemed to her to be ill with suppressed grief.

As for François, his trouble, so far from being less

as it appeared, grew daily. He thought of nothing else, and, sleeping or waking, far or near, Madeleine was always in his thoughts and her image before his eyes. It is true that all his life had been passed in loving and thinking of her. But until this time the thought had been pleasurable and comforting instead of sheer misery and disquietude. He had been so content to be her son and her friend that he had not wished for anything more ; but his love had changed in character and he was most unhappy.

He feared she could never change like him. He kept reminding himself that he was too young, that she had known him as a miserable child, and that he had caused her too much suffering and been too great a nuisance to the poor woman ; he feared that rather than feeling proud of him she regarded him with pity and compassion. In addition, she was so lovely and kind in his eyes, so far above him, and so desirable, that when she said she was no longer young or beautiful he thought that she did this in order to prevent him from courting her.

Since, however, Madame Sévère and Mariette with their friends were destroying her reputation on his account he began to be afraid lest the scandal might reach Madeleine's ears, that she might be annoyed about it and want to send him away. He said to himself that she was too good-natured to ask him to go, but that she would continue to suffer on his account as she had done before ; so he determined to go and ask the curé of Aigurande for his advice on the matter, knowing him to be a just and God-fearing man.

He went, but could not find him as he had gone to

visit the bishop ; so François went to stay with Jean Vertaud for two or three days until the curé should return.

His old master was the same decent fellow and good friend as formerly, and he found that his daughter Jeannette was about to be married to a nice man for reasons other than adoration of him, but for whom she had considerably more esteem than dislike. This put François at his ease with her as he had not been before, and as the next day was a Sunday he talked to her for a long while and told her confidentially of all the misery from which he had been able to rescue Madame Blanchet.

As Jeannette was quite sharp enough to put two and two together she gathered that this friendship went a good deal deeper than the waif admitted. And suddenly she seized his arm and said to him :

" François, you must not hide things from me. Now I am sensible and you see that I am not ashamed to tell you that I thought more of you than you did of me. You knew it and you made no response to my advances. But you did not try to mislead me and you did not do what a good many people might have done in your place. For that conduct and for your faithfulness to the woman whom you love more than anyone, I admire you, and instead of denying my feelings for you I am glad to remember them. I expect you like me the better for having told you this, and you will do me the justice of recognising that I bear no grudge for your coldness. I would like to give you one more token of my esteem, and this is how it appears to me . . . you love Madeleine Blanchet not so much as a mother, but entirely as a woman who is young and agreeable to you and whose husband you hope to become."

"Oh!" said François, blushing like a girl, "I love her as my mother and respect her from my heart."

"I have no doubt of that," replied Jeannette, "but you love her in two ways, for your face betrays one while your words tell me the other. Oh, well, François, you dare not tell her that which you dared not confess to me, and you do not know if she will respond to your double way of loving."

Jeannette Vertaud spoke with such sweetness and sense, and showed such true friendship for François, that he had not the courage to tell a lie, and pressing her hand he told her that he looked upon her as his sister and that she was the only person in the world to whom he could reveal his secret.

Jeannette then asked him a number of questions and he answered truthfully and with assurance. She said to him:

"François, my friend, now I understand. I cannot know what Madeleine Blanchet feels, but I see that you could stay with her ten years without being bold enough to tell her what is on your mind. Well, I will find out for you and tell you what she feels. To-morrow my father, you and I will set out so that we may make her acquaintance and pay a friendly visit to the kind woman who brought up our friend François. You will take my father for a walk round the place as if to ask his advice, and I will stay and talk to Madeleine. I will go slowly and I will not tell her about your feelings until I am sure about hers."

François nearly fell on his knees before Jeannette

to thank her for her goodness, and then Jean Vertaud was consulted with the waif's permission.

They set off the next day, Jeannette riding behind her father, while François went on ahead an hour earlier to inform Madeleine of the visit.

François reached Cormouer in the dusk. He was caught in a storm on the way, but he did not mind, for he had great hope of what Jeannette might do, and his heart was lighter than at his departure.

Raindrops clung to the bushes, and the blackbirds sang like mad to greet the mocking glance flung them by the sun as he sank behind the hill of Grand-Corlay. The fledglings in chirping flocks fluttered from branch to branch as François passed and their twittering cheered his spirits. He thought of the time when as a child he sauntered, loitering and dreaming, through the meadows, whistling to attract the birds. And at that moment he noticed a bullfinch which circled round his head as if it were an emblem of luck and good fortune. That reminded him of an old song about a bullfinch and its young which Mother Zabelle used to croon in the ancient language of our country as a lullaby for him.

Madeleine had not expected him so early. She had even feared that he would not return at all, and seeing him she could not help running to him and kissing him, which made him blush so much that she was surprised. He informed her of the visitors who were on their way, and that she should not mind, for it seemed as if he was as frightened lest she should guess as he was unhappy that she did not, he hinted that Jean Vertaud had some thought of buying property in the district.

Then Madeleine began to prepare the best feast she could for François' friends.

Jeannette was the first to enter the house while her father took their horse round to the stable; and as soon as she saw Madeleine she felt a great affection for her which Madeleine reciprocated; and having shaken hands they kissed one another as if for the sake of their love for François. They began to talk without restraint as if they had known one another for a long time. The truth is that they were a pair of good worthy women. Jeannette could not help feeling a trifle distressed to see Madeleine so much loved by the man for whom she herself still felt affection, but she was not at all jealous and she felt comforted by the good deed she was about to do.

On her side Madeleine, seeing this girl so buxom and attractive, imagined that it must have been for love of her that François had been so sad, that she had agreed to marry him, and had come to tell her this. She did not feel jealous either for she had never thought of François except as she thought of her own child.

But before nightfall, after supper, when Vertaud, tired by the journey, went off to bed, Jeannette led Madeleine outside, telling François to keep out of the way a little with Jeannie, and to come back when she turned down her apron which was tucked up at one corner.

She executed her mission so cleverly that Madeleine had no chance to misunderstand. She was very much astonished as the story was told. At first she thought that it was another proof of François' good-nature, that he wished to still the evil tongues and to serve her all his life. And she would have refused, thinking that it was too great a sacrifice on the part of so young a man to marry a woman older than himself, that he would repent later on, and that he would not remain faithful to her without boredom and regret. But Jeannette informed her that the waif was in love with her so deeply that his health and peace of mind were affected.

Madeleine found it difficult to believe, for she had lived so retired and chaste a life, never flirting or appearing outside her home or listening to compliments, that she had no idea that she was likely to be attractive in the eyes of a young man.

" And," Jeannette added, " since he finds you so agreeable, and since he will die of grief if you refuse him, will you continue to misunderstand and not to believe that which you are told ? If you do, it must be because you dislike the poor child and have no wish to make him happy."

" Don't say that, Jeannette," cried Madeleine, " I love him nearly as much, if not quite as much as my Jeannie, and if I had guessed that he loved me in another way I would not, as you can imagine, have been so placid in my friendship. But I had no idea of anything of the kind, and I am still so dazed that I do not know how to answer you. I implore you to give me time to think and to talk to him so that I may be sure it is no passing infatuation, or a result of being crossed in some other love, or even because he thinks it is his duty—for that is what I am most afraid of, and I feel he has rewarded me sufficiently for the care I took of him and that to give me himself as well as his freedom would be too much unless he really loves me as you imagine."

On hearing that Jeannette let fall her apron, and
François, who was not far distant and was watching
her, came towards them. Jeannette tactfully asked
Jeannie to show her the fountain, and they went off
leaving Madeleine and François together.

But Madeleine who had thought she could question
the waif quite calmly felt suddenly tongue-tied and
confused like a fifteen-year-old girl. It is not age,
but innocence of mind and action which causes that
timidity so charming to see ; and François, seeing his
dear mother blushing and trembling like himself
guessed that was more in his favour than her usual
calm manner. He took her hand and then her arm,
but could say nothing to her. Still trembling, she
desired to go after Jeannie and Jeannette, but he
held her back and made her turn round with him.
And Madeleine, feeling that his will made him bold
and able to overcome her resistance, realised better
than by words that it was no longer her child, the waif,
but her lover, François, who was walking by her
side.

When they had gone a little way without speaking,
but arm-in-arm and as close as possible, François
said to her :

" Let us go to the fountain—perhaps I shall find my
tongue there."

At the fountain they found no Jeannette and no
Jeannie, for they had gone in ; but François found
courage to speak, remembering that it was there he
had met Madeleine the first time, and there that he had
said farewell to her eleven years later.

It seems that he spoke well and that Madeleine did
not refuse him, for they were still there at midnight,

she weeping for joy, and he thanking her on his knees for consenting to accept him as her husband.

.   .   .   .   .   .

"That is the end of the story," said the hemp-dresser, "for the wedding is too long to tell about. I was there, and the same day that the waif married Madeleine in the parish of Mers, Jeannette also was married in the parish of Aigurande. And Jean Vertaud invited François and his wife and Jeannie, who was very glad about it all, with their friends, relatives, and acquaintances, to his house for the wedding feast, which was the finest and most delightful I have ever attended."

"Then it is a true story all through?" asked Sylvine Courtioux.

"If it is not, it might well have been," replied the hemp-dresser, "but if you don't believe me, go and see."